THE MARKS
of a CULT

David Breese

HARVEST HOUSE PUBLISHERS
Eugene, Oregon 97402

Verses marked NASB are taken from the New American Standard Bible, © 1960, 1962, 1963, 1968, 1971, 1972, 1973, 1975, 1977 by The Lockman Foundation. Used by permission.

Cover design by DesignTeam, Grand Rapids, Michigan

THE MARKS OF A CULT
Copyright © 1998 by Dave Breese
Published by Harvest House Publishers
Eugene, Oregon 97402

Library of Congress Cataloging-in-Publication Data
  Breese, Dave, 1926–
    [Know the marks of cults]
    The marks of a cult / Dave Breese.
      p. cm.
    Originally published: Know the marks of cults. Wheaton, Ill.: Victor Books, 1975.
    ISBN 1-56507-818-7
    1. Sects—Controversial literature. 2. Cults—Controversial literature. I. Title.
  BR157.B73 1998
  239'.9—dc21   97-44716
                                                  CIP

98 99 00 01 02 03 04 /BP/ 10 9 8 7 6 5 4 3 2 1

*To my daughter, Lynn,
with love,
hope,
and prayer.*

Contents

Acknowledgments

I wish to express my sincere thanks to faithful people who have rendered valuable aid. The first among these is Elmer Flaming, friend and father-in-law, who gave me the initial encouragement that it always takes to get a writing project underway. I am grateful also to Jackie Maplesden for her tireless research of the Los Angeles press, to Luella Yoder for her patient compilation of the tiresome cult pronouncements, and to Ruth Friesen and Carla Koslowsky for research, compilation, and manuscript preparation—all efforts beyond the call of duty.

The ideas and thoughts in this manuscript were greatly influenced by conversations with faithful pastors, youth directors, and Christian workers with whom I have had the blessed opportunity to serve in the ministry of evangelism across the world. They are a noble group who are carrying on the battle for truth in the front lines of today's spiritual conflict. God bless them all.

From the Author

It all started at a wedding.

Knowing I would have to sit in silence for 10 or 20 minutes before the ceremony and an equal time after, I took with me a small pamphlet about one of the cults. I read the helpful pages with interest and profit. The reading of the pamphlet, however, reminded me that it would take a whole library of books to analyze in detail each of the strange religions attracting people in our time.

But what if one could present in simple, readable fashion the marks that characterize the entire gamut of individual cults? That could be eminently helpful! That same evening I made notes of the general cult characteristics that I had observed. The result of those notes was a pamphlet entitled *The Marks of a Cult,* which has been distributed by the tens of thousands across America and on many overseas mission fields. The response from Christian leaders, pastors, radio broadcasters, and individual readers was most encouraging. Many requested additional material on the subject of the common religious heresies that are becoming fashionable today.

The editors at Victor Books indicated their interest in the expanded material. They requested a full manuscript on the subject, expressing the conviction that a study of these doctrinal principles would be helpful to churches, Sunday schools, and Christians across the world. Their encouragement was decisive. Then my friends at Harvest House Publishers decided to pick it up, and the results are before you on these pages.

I invite responsible correspondence by those who would present questions, suggestions, or further illustrations of the points contained herein. This material is written with the hope and prayer that it will glorify our only

Lord and Savior, Jesus Christ, and advance His gospel in these days in which truth is being challenged on every hand.

—Dave Breese
Christian Destiny
Hillsboro, Kansas

Deviation

A bias on the lines of life
Seems always to be there,
Slightly warping everything
The thickness of a hair.
It even turns the ship of state
By just a few degrees.
Anon the vessel founders low
In poorly charted seas.

Just so, in every deviant thought
The warp of truth is found,
To subtly ease the well-steered helm
To finally run aground.
The open seas must be achieved
Ere sails can be unfurled.
Then charted, tested truth will give
The vessel to the world.

Full many a man and many a cause
Embarked with noble goals.
But inattention to the helm
Wrought wreckage on the shoals.
Beware therefore the warp of life
That bends us from the plan.
With chart and compass stay the course.
At stake? The soul of man.

—Dave Breese

Moving Beyond Christianity

We are living in a day when many people are attempting to move "beyond" Christianity. Because of the myths of progress in vogue today, the word *beyond* has a certain appeal. Something that is forever fixed and changeless seems, in the minds of some, to be stodgy and undynamic. In this existential age, things must forever progress, fueled by the dynamism of some newly discovered life-force. The prevailing emotion of this civilization is not love or hate or anything so active—it is boredom. We demand new fascinations to feed our ever-shortening attention spans.

This demand for new ideas has led many to try to move past the faith once delivered to the saints to something newer (and therefore presumably truer) and more exciting. But the craving for something new is misguided. I will always be grateful for the words of Dr. Eastburg, my philosophy professor at Northern Seminary, who stated, "If it's new, it isn't true; and if it's true, it isn't new."

The Christian faith is the highest peak, everything else is downhill no matter which way one goes. There is nothing greater, nothing higher, and certainly nothing more magnificent than the divine revelation in Scripture and in Jesus Christ. To move beyond that mountaintop in the pursuit of something "better" is to lose oneself in the crags and crevices that fall away from real Christianity. And past the fissures of heresy are the fever swamps of cults, where the serpents and the scorpions await. Beyond love is lust, beyond sex is perversion, beyond medicine is poison, beyond fascination is addiction, beyond rationality is insanity, and beyond reality is fantasy. In the same way, beyond Christianity is death, darkness, and hopelessness.

Nevertheless, people continue to be offered those side paths whose ultimate direction is downward. The increasingly complicated religious situation of our time is producing an explosion of the strangest religious concoctions ever brought to the mind of man. This book is presented with the hope and prayer that it will help you identify those errors most characteristic of the cults in our time. It isn't really a study of the cults themselves; they are deserving of no such attention. This text is rather an expression of hope that we may develop the spiritual facility to instantly spot *the marks of the cults.* This will save us the bother and expense of further involvement. We must also realize that the same characteristics of religions that are out-and-out cults can begin within the true church of Christ. The recognition of those attributes that may be cultic, coupled with their early correction, may prevent future spiritual tragedy.

Writing to the Corinthians, the apostle Paul suggested that the believers examine themselves to be sure they are "in the faith" (2 Corinthians 13:5). This admonition, along with the warning that in latter times some shall depart from the faith (1 Timothy 4:1), should be cause enough for each of us to make careful doctrinal examination of himself. The clear teaching of Scripture is that if we would judge ourselves, we would not be judged by God (1 Corinthians 11:31,32). When one corrects his course in time, he shortens the process of sometimes painful spiritual correction. The absence of doctrinal correction produces spiritual ruin. How many disillusioned Christians have stood amid the broken pieces of their shattered lives and moaned, "If only I had known. Why didn't someone warn me in time?"

It is my prayer that these pages will bring a timely warning.

Why Cults Prosper

"I am the lord of the universe!"

These words were spoken by a young guru on a tour of the United States as he addressed 30,000 adoring devotees in Houston, Texas. Onlookers watched with astonishment as his young followers prostrated themselves in worship before their "perfect master."

Many people, knowing of such spectacles, wonder about the astonishing rise of strange religious leaders in our time. They see otherwise rational acquaintances of theirs give themselves to a new religious fanaticism, professing ecstatic conversion to the cause of some flaming messiah who has helped them discover a "new and sacred" truth. A mounting number of evangelical Christian congregations are increasingly concerned over the disappearance from their midst of whole families who have slipped away from the faith into an unheard of religion. "What is going on in our time?" they ask. "What strange new cults are assaulting the minds of people?"

A cult is a religious perversion. It is a belief and practice centered in false doctrine in the world of religion that calls for devotion to a religious view or leader. It is an organized heresy. A cult may take many forms, but it is basically a religious movement that distorts or warps orthodox faith to the point where truth becomes perverted into a lie. It is impossible to define a cult except in contrast to the absolute standard of the teaching of Holy Scripture. When contrasted to biblical truth, a cult is seen to have distinguishing marks by which it can be labeled as fatally "sub-Christian."

There is no question that one of the most interesting and dangerous developments of our time is the rise of aberrant religions. The promoters of old and new cults are active, and their works are growing as never before. Emboldened by easy successes, they believe they can capture new multitudes of followers. The result is that millions of souls are being beguiled into following religious notions that are nothing but false and satanic. The old cults are experiencing a remarkable resurgence, and curious new "faiths" are spawning in profusion.

When people hear of the strange beliefs and practices of the cults that share in today's religious resurgence, they understandably ask, "Why are so many men and women attracted to those unorthodox spiritual leaders? Why do people come under the spell of their strange, suspicious practices? Why are young people particularly susceptible to their influence?"

In answering these questions, we must first remember the Bible predicts that true Christianity will be under the constant attack of those who would deny and destroy the faith. One of the most moving speeches in the New Testament is the apostle Paul's warning to the elders of the church at Ephesus when he said goodbye and urged them to take proper care of the church:

> Be on guard for yourselves and for all the flock, among which the Holy Spirit has made you overseers, to shepherd the church of God which He purchased with His own blood. I know that after my departure savage wolves will come in among you, not sparing the flock; and from among your own selves men will arise, speaking perverse things, to

draw away the disciples after them. Therefore be
on the alert, remembering that night and day for a
period of three years I did not cease to admonish
each one with tears (Acts 20:28-31).

Paul warned the Ephesian elders (and all subsequent
Christians) that they would be subject to the attack of the
enemy from two quarters: within and without. Grievous
wolves would come in from the outside, and those who
would appear to be members of the flock would arise from
the inside. Both were dangers to the flock. Because of this,
the elders were told that they must be on the alert. The
elders were never told they should be merely popular
leaders, fashioning a message that would promote con-
sensus among various points of view. Rather, they were to
be faithful custodians and teachers of the eternal, absolute
truth of God.

This commission to the elders of the early church is
surely valid for those who are custodians of the work of
God in our own age. Few question that we are living in the
day predicted by the apostle Paul when he said, "But the
Spirit explicitly says that in later times some will fall away
from the faith, paying attention to deceitful spirits and doctrines of demons" (1 Timothy 4:1). Why then are people
attracted to false religious doctrines and practices as
opposed to true commitment to Jesus Christ and His
church? A number of reasons for this spiritual defection are
given to us in the Word of God.

1. *Love of Darkness*

A person determined to live an immoral life, or even a
self-centered one, will flee from the truth of the gospel
when it shows his life for what it is—an offense to God.
People love darkness; they hate the light. One of the chief
reasons people refuse to believe the gospel of Christ after

they hear the truth is its ruthless illumination of sin and its call to repentance and faith in the Savior: "And this is the judgment, that the light is come into the world, and men loved the darkness rather than the light; for their deeds were evil. For everyone who does evil hates the light, and does not come to the light, lest his deeds should be exposed. But he who practices the truth comes to the light, that his deeds may be manifested as having been wrought in God" (John 3:19-21).

Similarly, one of the primary reasons professing Christians defect from their allegiance to Christ is that they have fallen into sin and refuse to return to fellowship with God on the basis of repentance and faith. Since "everyone who does evil hates the light," they will continue to walk in and love the darkness. While doing so, the sinner imagines that his evil deeds are unknown to God and to his fellowman. Nothing could be more foolish! No one can hide his thoughts or actions from the God who sees everything. As the writer to the Hebrews put it, "There is no creature hidden from His sight, but all things are open and laid bare to the eyes of Him with whom we have to do" (Hebrews 4:13).

Despite this fact, there are those who go on refusing to recognize the moral law of God. They choose to embrace a false doctrine that excuses their immoral or self-centered lives, preferring the temporal pleasures of sin and self-will to the joy of Christ's forgiveness and eternal life. Often this kind of person is lured into a false religion. Though its requirements may be silent, he can still retain his rebellion against God—or at least an independence from Him. The person feels he can still go his own way without experiencing eternal consequences. His love of darkness blinds him from the truth.

2. *Spiritual Immaturity*

The period in our Christian lives when we are most vulnerable to the subversion of false doctrine is when we are in spiritual infancy. When we step out of darkness into the light of the gospel, believing in Jesus Christ, we are justified by faith. At that point we become what Scripture calls a "newborn babe" (1 Peter 2:2). Few eras in our Christian lives will be so fresh, so beautiful, and so thoroughly enjoyable. Our testimonies will probably reveal the ecstasies that are now ours in knowing Jesus Christ. Many a Christian hymn writer has expressed the delight of the heart that has discovered the reality of salvation in Christ. Everything is different, as Robinson suggests:

> *Heav'n above is softer blue,*
> *Earth around is sweeter green!*
> *Something lives in every hue*
> *Christless eyes have never seen:*
> *Birds with gladder songs o'erflow,*
> *Flow'rs with deeper beauties shine,*
> *Since I know, as now I know,*
> *I am His, and He is mine.*

Like children of the flesh, spiritual babies are a precious treasure to their Father. Few things delight our Lord more than the simple trust of a just-born Christian. This is a time of rejoicing in heaven and of personal joy in the heart of the believer. But this is also a time of great danger. The spiritual infant must not tarry too long in infancy, supinely savoring his happiness in Christ. He must proceed as quickly as possible to a program of spiritual growth. Otherwise he will be in great jeopardy from the hostile environment of the world. Many childhood diseases can overtake the newborn babe in the family of God, and one of the most dangerous is involvement with cults.

In our time we can see the happy results of evangelism in the lives of millions who have come to faith in Jesus Christ. The great and commendable efforts of the church and its gifted workers have produced many thousands of new converts to the Lord Jesus. The result is that there are great numbers of spiritual infants in the church. Knowing this, the cults are thriving by pressing an ambitious program of deceptive practices against these blessed newborn souls, using the deadly virus of false and destructive heresies.

It follows, therefore, that one of the great needs in the church today is for Christian growth. Nothing is more important than this in the life of the newborn Christian; he or she is called upon to "desire the sincere milk of the Word" that he or she may grow as a result. The key to the development of Christian maturity is given us by the apostle Paul in an admonition that should be heeded by us all: "All Scripture is inspired by God and profitable for teaching, for reproof, for correction, for training in righteousness; that the man of God may be adequate, equipped for every good work" (2 Timothy 3:16,17). The study of Holy Scripture and the consequent development toward spiritual maturity is imperative for the Christian.

What is the key to spiritual growth? It is the study of the Word of God that produces the knowledge of sound doctrine. What protects a new believer from the lure of a cult? A solid knowledge of God's Word, which equips him for serving the Lord.

3. *Spiritual Subversion*

Another reason sincere people are drawn into the cults is that traveling religious charlatans work industriously to subvert people from true faith in Jesus Christ. This was the case with a group of young Christians who had embraced the gospel under the ministry of the apostle Paul in the province of Galatia. Under his preaching they responded to the ministry of the grace of God with commendable enthusiasm. Thus Paul says, "I bear you witness, that if possible, you would have plucked out your eyes and given them to me" (Galatians 4:15). The ecstatic response of the people in Galatia to his preaching must have been a singular encouragement to the apostle. Therefore, we can understand the brokenness he must have felt as he wrote to those Galatian believers a short time later. He had heard of the spiritual subversion that was taking place in the lives of those beloved Christians, and he exclaimed,

> I am amazed that you are so quickly deserting Him who called you by the grace of Christ, for a different gospel; which is really not another; only there are some who are disturbing you, and want to distort the gospel of Christ. But even though we, or an angel from heaven, should preach to you a gospel contrary to that which we have preached to you, let him be accursed. As we have said before, so I say again now, if any man is preaching to you a gospel contrary to that which you received, let him be accursed (Galatians 1:6-9).

It seems that certain representatives had come from Jerusalem to conduct a follow-up ministry among the Galatians. They doubtless commended the Galatians for believing in the gospel of the grace of God, but then proceeded to insist that they must become obedient to the law of Moses in order to be true Christians. Describing these leaders, Paul said, "They eagerly seek you, not commendably, but *they wish to shut you out,* in order that you may seek them" (Galatians 4:17, emphasis added). The apostle then admonished the Christians, "It was for freedom that Christ set us free; therefore keep standing firm and do not be subject again to a yoke of slavery" (Galatians 5:1). Thus did Paul resist the spiritual subverters that were entering like grievous wolves among the flock.

Spiritual subversion also took place among the Corinthians. The Christians at Corinth were also spiritually immature (see 1 Corinthians 3:1). As babes in Christ, they were vulnerable to those ubiquitous spiritual carpetbaggers that moved in to make merchandise of them. The subverters of the Corinthian church were advocating the heresy of *phenomenalism*—that is, they were denying the biblical thesis that "the just shall live by faith" and insisting that "the just shall live by sight." Concerning these enemies of the faith, Paul wrote, "Such men are false apostles, deceitful workers, disguising themselves as apostles of Christ. And no wonder, for even Satan disguises himself as an angel of light. Therefore, it is not surprising if his servants also disguise themselves as servants of righteousness; whose end shall be according to their deeds" (2 Corinthians 11:13-15).

Following this, Paul, with a sense of astonishment states, "For you bear with anyone if he enslaves you, if he devours you, if he takes advantage of you, if he exalts himself, if he hits you in the face" (2 Corinthians 11:20). In other words, the apostle was amazed at the beating the Christians were allowing themselves to go through by these false teachers. In this passage he is speaking against the terrible spiritual vulnerability of infantile Christians. Being weak and spineless, they allowed themselves to be knocked around and exploited by every new spiritual pretender who moved into their midst.

The church at Colossae was also the object of spiritual exploiters attempting to corrupt the theology at this outpost of Christian liberty. The troublemakers came preaching the mysterious Gnostic heresy, claiming that a deeper knowledge freed them from having to obey Christ's call to righteousness. Paul said, "See to it that no one takes you captive through philosophy and empty deception, according to the tradition of men, according to the elementary principles of the world, rather than according to Christ" (Colossians 2:8). He followed up these words with the warning: "Let no one keep defrauding you of your prize by delighting in self-abasement and the worship of the angels, taking his stand on visions he has seen, inflated without cause by his fleshly mind" (Colossians 2:18).

During the apostolic era, it is probable that no church in the New Testament escaped the dreadful attention of the traveling servants of Satan, who saw in these young congregations the opportunity to operate like disguised wolves in a sheepfold. We may be sure that few churches in our present day will escape the like attention of similar spiritual opportunists.

4. *Intellectual Pride*

Another cause for defection from Christ and involvement in false religion is that pride of intellect to which any of us may be susceptible. This attitude among the Corinthians made it easier for the spiritual subverters to steal their affections from Christ. Paul once wrote:

> But I am afraid, lest as the serpent deceived Eve by his craftiness, your minds should be led astray from the simplicity and purity of devotion to Christ. For if one comes and preaches another Jesus whom we have not preached, or you receive a different spirit which you have not received, or a different gospel which you have not accepted, you bear this beautifully (2 Corinthians 11:3,4).

The gospel is supposed to be believed with "simplicity and godly sincerity," he told the Corinthians. We don't come to know Christ because of our great wisdom, but because of the grace of God. Unfortunately, intellectual pride has led many to feel that Christianity is "not sophisticated enough" or is "too simple" for their perceptive intellects. They are embarrassed at the invitation to come as little children to Christ and to continue to be humble seekers after truth. They are "vainly puffed up in their own fleshly minds," as was the case with some of those in the Colossian church. Such people resent the Scripture that says: "For it is written, 'I will destroy the wisdom of the wise, and the cleverness of the clever I will set aside.' Where is the wise man? Where is the scribe? Where is the debater of this age? Has not God made foolish the wisdom of the world? For since in the wisdom of God the world through its wisdom did not come to know God, God was well-pleased through the foolishness of the message preached to save those who believe" (1 Corinthians 1:19-21).

True wisdom consists of simple obedience to God and His Word. Each of us does well never to forget the advice of Job, the wise patriarch of the Old Testament who said, "Behold, the fear of the Lord, that is wisdom; and to depart from evil is understanding" (Job 28:28). Nevertheless, the fact remains that for these and many other reasons the cults continue to grow in numbers and influence in western civilization. Volumes could be written to analyze the distinctive delusions of the nearly endless list of individual cults. Surely the better course would be to consider the typical deficiencies of these groups. With these in mind, we will better recognize a cult, however new, as being a religious deviation condemned in Scripture.

5. *Outright Satanic Activity*

When thinking of anything in today's temporal world, there is an influence we must not forget—his infernal majesty, the devil. The arrangements that we make in life or the trouble which comes to us is not simply of mechanical or accidental origin. It could be that we are being confronted by outright satanic activity. We have a statement of Satan's primary concern given to us in the Word of God. Paul, describing his work, also detailed the labor of Satan to hinder the gospel:

> Therefore, since we have this ministry, as we received mercy, we do not lose heart, but we have renounced the things hidden because of shame, not walking in craftiness or adulterating the word of God, but by the manifestation of truth commending ourselves to every man's conscience in the sight of God. And even if our gospel is veiled, it is veiled to those who are perishing, in whose case the god of this world has blinded the minds of the unbelieving, that they might not see the light of the gospel of the glory of Christ, who is the image of God (2 Corinthians 4:3,4).

Satan's primary interest is to deny or obscure the truth of God so that salvation will seem unobtainable to many who would otherwise believe. This is a continued and purposeful activity on the part of the devil. Therefore, Scripture warns us to "be of sober spirit, be on the alert. Your adversary, the devil, prowls about like a roaring lion, seeking someone to devour. But resist him, firm in your faith, knowing that the same experiences of suffering are being accomplished by your brethren who are in the world" (1 Peter 5:8).

To emphasize the seriousness of satanic activity, the Word of God gives us further warning. In the last days satanic activity will heighten. Satan and his minions will work overtime to subvert the truth. "Woe to the earth and the sea," it says in Revelation 12:12, "because the devil has come down to you, having great wrath, knowing that he has only a short time."

There will come a time in which satanic activity will greatly expand in size and in fury as we move into the last days. Iniquity is progressive. We can, therefore, expect a marked increase in the proclamations of false doctrine, the rise of the cults, and the multiplication of aberrant religions in our time. The devil is the chief promoter of false doctrine in our world. Frantically he moves to accomplish this mission in his perverse life.

Satanic blindness can be expected to lend new force to the cultic expansion. We need not be surprised at a cultic expansion moving upon our churches and Christian institutions in these difficult days. When we realize that some of this neo-satanic activity comes from within the ranks of the religious community, we should recognize it as a predicted sign of the times. Satan is bent on the destruction of the church, and his demons are laboring to disrupt and disturb Christians.

Those who have been involved in a cult have frequently testified to the horror of their involvement. For example, David Berkowitz, the "Son of Sam" who murdered six people in New York City in the 1980's, was recently featured on a television program. Since the dreadful days in which he spent his nights prowling the streets for victims, he now professes to have become a born-again Christian. On the show Berkowitz testified, "The average person has no idea as to the compelling influence that comes into a life when one is dedicated to do the will of Satan." He went on to say that it seemed as if another personality had taken over his life and was compelling him to do evil. In the process, he also insisted that there are many more totally satanic cults than the average person realizes. Berkowitz warns that to toy with satanic symbolism is a very dangerous practice.

Dealing with the devil is thought of as being fun and games to many a young person. Often mere curiosity will lead an impressionable boy or girl into a cult that may be satanic. What was curiosity fulfillment at the beginning becomes the path to a depraved life . . . and often a most horrible death. It is a very serious undertaking to follow a leader who professes to be God or a special representative of God. One of Satan's main interests is personal aggrandizement, and he can be counted on to exalt himself on many occasions. His devices may include homosexuality, pedophilia, debasing sexual experiences, and drugs—the very soul-destroying practices that have flourished in our culture.

Satanic cults are reported to be growing remarkably, and making more and more unspeakable demands in the lives of their followers. This has come, some people testify, to the level of ritual murder and every ghastly practice that may grow out of dedication to the devil. When the Bible testifies that "evil men and impostors will proceed from bad to worse, deceiving and being deceived" (2 Timothy 3:13), it is certainly offering a warning most applicable to our time.

There are not enough hours in one lifetime to read all the material being produced by those who believe something other than the gospel of Jesus Christ. However, one does not need to do this. All one must do is examine the Scriptures and hold any teaching of the cults up to the light of God's Word. The first responsibility each Christian has is not to be an expert on the cults, but on the Word of God. Few pursuits are more exhausting than the attempt to get to the bottom of the endless labyrinth of cult pronouncements. One may avoid this pointless activity by remembering that if a religious view bears the characteristics that are described in this book, it does not merit further study and can be dismissed as another gospel, not true biblical faith. A cultic religious point of view may be positive in many ways—and even true in part. That's what makes it attractive to its followers. What makes a religious practice a cult, however, is not only the false teachings that it professes, but also its fatal omissions of sound doctrine.

STUDY QUESTIONS

1. How would you define a cult?

2. Why do you think people are attracted to cults?

3. Why are new Christians particularly susceptible to being ensnared by cults?

4. How can spiritual pride get in the way of spiritual development?

5. What advice would you give to someone who asks, "How can I experience spiritual growth?"

Beyond the Bible

How has God revealed Himself?

The Christian answer to that question is that God has been revealed in many ways in days gone by. In these last days, God "has spoken to us in His Son, whom He appointed heir of all things, through whom also He made the world" (see Hebrews 1:1,2). The Almighty has shown Himself fully and finally to all mankin in Jesus Christ, as revealed in the Word of God.

The Bible is God's final and complete revelation, and this revelation can be supplanted by no other. The cults have no such commitment, believing in the heretical doctrine of extrabiblical revelation. They claim that God has spoken and recorded words through any number of mediums, asserting that the Lord speaks or has spoken outside or apart from the Bible. In other words, to the cults, the New Testament Scriptures are not complete.

The first and most typical characteristic of a cult is that *it claims for its authority some revelation apart from the clear statements of the Word of God.* Most cults claim to respect the teachings of the Bible, and many even attribute divine inspiration to Holy Scripture. But they quickly announce their real confidence in some subsequent revelation they claim is more authoritative than God's Word. This, in effect, cancels the teaching of the Bible. Many cults claim that the Bible is only *part* of the verbal revelation of God.

One Los Angeles-based religious cult recently adver-
tised:

> The Bible has become to you the Book, but I would
> also have you know that God has inspired men and
> women with power to reveal, in our own time, even
> greater things, and ever fresh unfoldings from the
> heart of life.

> Above all things, we want you to have the open
> vision today, for greater things are coming, and
> God is doing wonders among you. Rejoice in the
> new revelation, abounding in hope. The new will
> reveal the old to you afresh. Have no doubts.
> Launch out into the deeps of God, and fear not.
> Eternity is now.

Sometimes this extrabiblical revelation comes in the
form of a "divinely inspired leader." Many religions have
invested divine authority in the person of a visible individual who claims infallibility, his words having the same or
higher authority than Holy Scripture. From "Brother Julius"
in Brooklyn, to a spiritual temple in Los Angeles, the cults
continue to press for a "better" revelation than the Word of
God. William Branham, in his *Word to the Bible,* said, "One
night as I was seeking the Lord, the Holy Spirit told me to
pick up my pen and write. As I grasped the pen to write, His
Spirit gave me a message for the church. I want to bring it
to you. . . . It has to do with the Word and the bride." The
Bible apparently not being enough, the cults look for extrabiblical teachings to support their heretical ideas.

The God of the Bible, knowing this would be the case in
the future of the church, very clearly declares His Word, the
Bible, to be the final and complete revelation. It cannot be
superseded. After giving us 66 books in the Old and New
Testaments, the Holy Spirit directed the apostle John to categorically close the verbal revelation of God at the end of

the Bible text, saying, "I testify to everyone who hears the words of the prophecy of this book: if anyone adds to them, God shall add to him the plagues which are written in this book; and if anyone takes away from the words of the book of this prophecy, God shall take away his part from the tree of life and from the holy city, which are written in this book" (Revelation 22:18,19). Clearly then, we have in Scripture a dreadful curse placed upon anyone who presumes to present a new verbal revelation from God.

In a frantic attempt at rationalization, some cultists say, "Well, our revelation did not come from the word of man but from a higher source." (The Mormons' claim to the coming of an angel is an illustration of this.) As if foreseeing this, the apostle Paul wrote, "But even though we, or an angel from heaven, should preach to you a gospel contrary to that which we have preached to you, let him be accursed. As we have said before, so I say again now, if any man is preaching to you a gospel contrary to that which you received, let him be accursed"(Galatians 1:8,9). The early church wasn't interested in any messages that went beyond the Bible—they wanted the truth, the whole truth, and nothing but the truth.

The Revelation of Jesus Christ

The cults usually claim that their messages are something special God has revealed to them in a supernatural way. They'll even refer to Scripture as an example of God offering messages directly to man. It is true that in biblical times the Word was carried to man by angels (see Hebrews 2:2), but we are told in Scripture that the revelation of Jesus Christ supersedes this. Hebrews 1:1,2 reads, "God, after He spoke long ago to the fathers in the prophets in many portions and in many ways, in these last days has spoken to us in His Son, whom He appointed heir of all things, through whom also He made the world."

Christ is better than the angels, and all of the angels of God are commanded to worship Him. The final words of Scripture, "the Revelation of Jesus Christ," can never be superseded by the ministry of angels. This is why Jesus Christ advised His disciples and us to "continue in My word" (John 8:31). Our present age is also well advised to heed the words of the Father, who not only said, "This is My beloved Son, with whom I am well-pleased," but also added the command, "Listen to Him" (Matthew 17:5).

It is a cardinal doctrine of Christianity that final truth, the ultimate word, is resident in Jesus Christ. Indeed, the Scripture is even stronger than that, proclaiming, "In the beginning was the Word, and the Word was with God, and the Word *was* God" (John 1:1, emphasis added). Final truth, therefore, is the person, the word, and the work of Jesus Christ. No subsequent revelation as to the nature of truth can supersede His revelation. It is simply impossible for there to be a greater message in the universe than that of Christ. There is no better word from the God who made this world.

Equal to Scripture?

One frequent device of a cult is to lend credence to its own writings by placing them parallel to God's Word, then moving them up to a greater authority, as in this example:

> The revealed scriptures predict the genuine incarnations of God well in advance of their earthly appearances. For instance, the Old Testament predicted the appearance of Lord Jesus Christ, and Srimad Bhagavatam predicted the appearance of Lord Buddha, Lord Caitanya Mahaprabhu, and even Lord Kam, who will not appear for another 400,000

years. Without reference to such bona fide scriptural predictions, no incarnation of the Lord can be
bona fide. Indeed, the scriptures warn that in this
age there will be many false incarnations. Lord
Jesus Christ cautioned his followers that in the
future many impostors would claim to be him. Similarly, Srimad-Bhagavatam also warns of false incarnations, describing them to be just like glowworms
imitating the moon. Modern impostors often claim
that their ideas represent the same teachings
taught by Christ or Krishna, but anyone truly
familiar with the teachings of Christ or Krishna can
easily see that this is just nonsense.[1]

So it is that the Krishna cult, the modern followers of
His Divine Grace A.C. Bhaktivedanta Swami Prabhupada,
grasp for authority in the minds of the confused. They place
their arcane and mysterious writings on a par with Scripture.

A word of admonition is in order. The Christian believes
the Bible to be *the final and only verbal revelation of God.*
Believing this, he must give himself to the study of the Word
of God with a higher degree of intensity than ever before.
The subtle assaults being leveled against the Scripture in
these days need to be answered by articulate Christians in
all walks of life. It is not enough for us to hold the Bible in
tranquil veneration, looking at it with great admiration as
the touchstone of our faith. The Bible is "the sword of the
Spirit" and will become an effective instrument against
satanic assaults when we build the teaching of Holy Scripture into the very fiber of our beings.

We are being inconsistent and perhaps hypocritical if
we profess a high view of Scripture but neglect to dispel
our own lack of understanding of the truth of God through
a serious program of Bible study. I believe the greatest

single reason for the advance of the cults in our world today is ignorance of Holy Scripture on the part of Christians. The second greatest reason is unwillingness on the part of the people of God to transmit divine truth by way of a testimony for Christ to others who need to receive salvation in Christ.

It follows that the great need in the Christian community is a return to the careful study of the Word of God. Faith that the Bible is ultimate truth will come from that very program of Bible reading. A study of Scripture will produce in the life of the Christian the fulfillment of the promise, "Faith comes from hearing, and hearing by the word of Christ" (Romans 10:17).

It is well known that truth bears its own credentials to the honest mind. No one will doubt the final authority of the Word of God if he gives himself to the attentive study of Bible doctrine and Scripture memorization. David hid the Word of God in his heart in order to resist the sinful alternatives of life (see Psalm 119:11). This means he memorized portions of the Bible, and so should we. The life of a Christian will be firmly anchored against all opposition when it is grounded in a working knowledge of Holy Scripture. The fearful assault upon the church by aroused and powerful cults will be withstood only when Christians are made strong in the Lord by knowledge of His Word.

Spiritual Seduction

One of the oft-repeated questions in life should certainly be, "By what authority?" There are a thousand voices calling us to allegiance. These voices are saying, "Follow me," "Believe my message," and "I am the one with a final word for you." We can be sure that the volume of such voices will increase as we move toward the end of the age. The Bible promises that "in later times some will fall away from the faith, paying attention to deceitful spirits and doctrines of demons," or, as the King James Version puts it, "seducing spirits." The Scripture warns us of a very pernicious influence that will come upon the world and upon the church during the last days as people pay more attention to the lies of Satan.

Shall we believe these voices that come shouting into our ears? Millions will impute to these voices some kind of a sublime authority. Many shall follow the destructive ways of these false prophets, gullibly believing an alternative claim to truth that is nothing more than empty air. It's interesting to note the reason people will be so attracted to these voices: They will have been seduced by the doctrines of demons.

What is the goal of spiritual seduction? It is to lure people from the path of rectitude with the promise of physical ecstasy. Demons, therefore, are working to produce a warm and wonderful physical ecstasy along with promoting false doctrines. There will be lights, color, laughter, throbbing music, and a dozen other feel-good phenomena along with the heretical preaching. So it is that today so many people claim truth for their ideas simply because of their testimony. "It felt good," we are told. "It really made me happy," they say, reasoning that their ecstasy therefore implies its truth. There is grave peril in believing a feel-good religion that uses one's feelings as the authority for their bizarre messages of "truth."

Satan and his demons will motivate more and more people to believe lies as we move toward the consummation of history. A demonic doctrine is a satanic lie that is presented as basic belief for Christian reality. There are ten very believable lies that Satan has planted in this world, and they have most certainly deceived many. These lies are:

1. God is a cosmic sadist.

2. God is a liar.

3. God is not worthy.

4. God should work miracles on demand.

5. This life is everything.

6. There is no destiny.

7. Exploit the promises of God.

8. Adversity will produce apostasy.

9. Satan's way is the best way.

10. Don't go to the cross.[2]

We can be sure that Satan will continue to perpetuate these cosmic falsehoods because they are effective in deceiving and winning the perverse commitment of many.

Every form of extrabiblical revelation is a lie. It is concocted in hell and delivered by well-meaning deceivers and outright cult promoters. The poet put it well when he said,

> *Mid sinking sands of doubt and fear*
> *There is the one foundation stone*
> *My soul has cast her anchor here*
> *I rest upon thy Word alone.*

As I've mentioned before, one of the most important questions that needs to be asked is, "By what authority do you speak?" In answer to that question some will say, "I speak by the authority of the church." The church is the body of Christ, established by the authority of the Word of God being preached. The church *isn't* the final authority; the Word of God *is*. Others will claim, "I stand for the truth of my tradition." Among the older denominations—and perhaps some of the newer ones—this is a popular point of view. But when the traditions of sinful man supersede the authority of the Word of God, then one can predict the future inch by inch and hour by hour. The Word of God will be relegated to a peripheral position, and human wisdom will take its place. The result will be a destruction of faith and a rejection of God. The collapse of our major liberal denominations, the mainline churches often called the "seven sisters," is a perfect example. As they have moved away from Scripture, they have seen steady decline.

Christian, beware of extrabiblical revelations. It turns churches into humanistic cults where the Word of God is soon a forgotten commodity.

STUDY QUESTIONS

1. According to Romans 1:18,20 and Hebrews 1:1,2, how has God revealed Himself?

2. What does Revelation 22:18,19 have to say about the Bible being the complete revelation of God?

3. What response would you give to someone who claimed to have received a new revelation?

4. "The single greatest reason for the advance of the cults in our world today is ignorance of the Holy Scripture on the part of Christians." Do you agree or disagree? Why?

5. How do you see the ten "doctrines of demons" promoted in our culture?

Chasing After Salvation

What must I do to be saved?

Deep within his heart, every person on earth is asking that question first phrased by the Philippian jailer. We are born with an unquenchable longing for eternal life and a home in heaven that will never pass away. Millions of people may never admit to this desire, but within each soul is the constantly pressing wish for a secure eternal reality— a hope that goes beyond the grave. This longing is the fuel that energizes the growth of most of the cults in existence today. Because they are involved in some form of exploitation, the cults without exception obscure the truth and chase after salvation on a basis other than the free gift that comes to us by the grace of God.

What is the true basis of salvation? The clear teaching of the New Testament is that eternal salvation comes to a believer solely as a result of faith in Jesus Christ. The Scriptures declare again and again this sublime Christian truth: "Therefore having been justified by faith, we have peace with God through our Lord Jesus Christ, through whom also we have obtained our introduction by faith into this grace in which we stand; and we exult in hope of the glory of God" (Romans 5:12).

Salvation: A Free Gift

Consider the testimony of Paul in his letter to the Romans. He notes, for example, that "all have sinned and fall short of the glory of God, being justified as a gift by His grace through the redemption which is in Christ Jesus" (Romans 3:23,24). Paul went on to note that "to the one who works, his wage is not reckoned as a favor, but as what is due. But to the one who does not work, but believes in Him who justifies the ungodly, his faith is reckoned as righteousness" (4:4,5). We do not *earn* our salvation. Eternal life is a *gift* from God, given to those who put their faith in Him. Therefore "a man is justified by faith apart from works of the Law" (3:28).

These and many other clear declarations of the New Testament positively establish the basis of salvation to be the finished work of Christ alone and our faith in that work. Paul once wrote to the believers in Galatia and declared, "A man is not justified by the works of the Law but through faith in Christ Jesus, even we have believed in Christ Jesus, that we may be justified by faith in Christ, and not by the works of the Law; since by the works of the Law shall no flesh be justified" (Galatians 2:16). And in Ephesians 2:8,9, he reminds us, "For by grace you have been saved through faith; and that not of yourselves, it is the gift of God; not as a result of works, that no one should boast." The Bible is clear regarding how we are saved, and it is not earned by our good works.

By contrast, Scripture teaches that all other forms of supposed salvation, based on human efforts, are cursed by God: "For as many as are of the works of the Law are under a curse; for it is written, 'Cursed is everyone who does not abide by all things written in the book of the law, to perform them.' Now that no one is justified by the Law before God is evident; for, 'The righteous man shall live by faith'" (Galatians 3:10,11).

How wonderful is the message of the gospel of the grace of God presented to us in Holy Scripture! A person is able to come to Jesus Christ without money, without human works, without vast promises concerning the future. He can accept salvation entirely purchased for him on the cross. When he comes in humble faith, he receives the gift of God, which is eternal life. And it is exactly that: a free gift. When he believes the gospel, he receives eternal life and is justified in the sight of God.

To be justified, of course, means to be *declared* righteous. This is a legal change in the attitude of God toward the sinner, and it depends on the saving act of Jesus Christ. It is entirely independent of the experience of the believer. The wonderful change which may result in a believer's life is not itself salvation, but rather the human and variable *result* of that saving faith. Eternal salvation comes to the believer because of imputed righteousness. Imputed righteousness is righteousness that is placed in his account in heaven. Christ has done the work, and He offers sinners a free gift.

The Grace of God

During the course of his or her Christian life, a person may develop a wonderful degree of personal righteousness. In this, he will have the powerful help of the indwelling Holy Spirit of God. The true believer can be expected to work toward perfect holiness in the fear of God, under the leadership of the Holy Spirit. Personal righteousness is not, however, the basis of salvation. He is saved on the basis of imputed righteousness. This comes to him as a free gift, already purchased by the enormous cost of the finished work of Christ on Calvary's cross. The Christian is saved, not because of his own works, but because of the saving work of Jesus Christ when He died—the just for the unjust—that He might bring us to God (1 Peter 3:18). The total benefits of Calvary come to the believer on the basis of grace.

That is crucial for us to remember: *It is the grace of God alone that brings salvation.*

No message is more viciously attacked by the cult promoters of our present world than the gospel of the grace of God. Those who would promote slavish religious systems are infuriated at the gracious offer of Jesus Christ to bring His life into the sin-darkened soul, and to do it without any form of payment. It is absolutely maddening to the professional religious promoters that God saves individuals freely, by grace alone.

No false religion in the world can possibly survive unless it is able to destroy the gospel of the grace of God and introduce or encourage a system of human works as a basis of salvation. There is not room in the same world for the plain message of justification by faith without the deeds of the law and the cultic religionist with his perverted gospel. Every cult in the world preaches "another gospel" and is therefore cursed of God. Nevertheless, cult promoters continue to press their malignant doctrines of other ways to salvation instead of faith in the finished work of Christ on the cross.

Salvation by Something Else

One of the most popular alternative doctrines of salvation is that of *salvation by membership*. Herbert W. Armstrong's Worldwide Church of God, now in repentance and returning to the faith, used to announce that the only saved people were those who were members of their religious establishment. Counterfeit Christianity in many forms has often announced that "there is no salvation outside of the church," meaning outside *their* religious syndicate. Failure to keep one's membership intact incurs the damnation of the soul.

Others offer even stranger salvation promises, such as *salvation by sublime association*. The new Krishna devotees are told:

> Therefore one who is sufficiently intelligent will associate with saintly persons who are free from the entanglement of material nature and who can sever the knots which bind. There is no benefit in associating with those who are simply engaged in sense gratification.

> If we want liberation, if we really want to get out of this illusory existence, we must associate with *mahatmas,* great souls. All we have to do is simply hear, *sravanam,* and by simply hearing from great souls our knot of nascence will be cut. Just hearing "Hare Krishna, Hare Krishna, Krishna Krishna, Hare Hare, Hare Rama, Hare Rama, Rama Rama, Hare Hare" will save us.[3]

Another alternative to the way of faith is the cult doctrine of *salvation by works*. In many of these religious programs, what a person *believes* is of little consequence; it is what he *does* that counts. The versions of this works doctrine are many. Some emphasize years of service, weekly hours spent in work, the giving of money, the practice of strange incantations, the reciting of chants—the list is endless. There is an immense number of possible obligations to which the soul enslaves itself when it turns from the divine offer of salvation by faith alone.

The followers of the Jehovah's Witnesses are told that the basis of judgment at the end of the 1,000 years will be solely the works they perform during the millennium. Christian Scientists are asked to believe that salvation consists of being saved from the illusions and delusions of mortal sense . . . the sense of becoming sick and dying.

In the early days of Mormonism, Mormon women accepted the staggering involvement in polygamy because they became convinced that their salvation depended on it. Unitarians believe in salvation by character, holding that man will find the road that leads to peace and brotherhood through development of "moral values and spiritual insights." The followers of Theosophy hold that man is saved by working out his own "kanna" or law works. What he is now is the result of previous works, and what he is to become is the result of his present works.

The list of those who are pursuing inner light, perfect realization, transcendental thoughts, or other baseless notions as they chase salvation is seemingly endless. All of these human works inevitably lead to despair.

By Grace Alone

By contrast to all of this, we need to hear again the finality of the words of Paul: "If righteousness comes through the Law, then Christ died needlessly" (Galatians 2:21). Proud men and women who still retain confidence in their abilities to do good things that will be pleasing to God and produce salvation need to be reminded of the words of Jesus Christ: "None of you carries out the Law" (John 7:19). We can seek God through our works, but we'll never find Him that way.

There is no question that every false cult will finally lead to human despair, death, and hell. Millions could be saved from this spiritual tragedy if they would turn in simple confidence to the promise of Scripture: "Believe on the Lord Jesus Christ, and you shall be saved" (Acts 16:31). Few scenes are more tragic than that of a benighted soul pursuing a false hope of salvation when Jesus Christ offers it as a free gift.

Let us then forever establish the proposition, the thrilling truth, that *salvation is by grace alone*. Still, in the midst of that obvious truth, there are those who place their faith in many other things and become tragic stories of spiritual ruin. One of the most common objects of faith is found in the statement, "My faith is in the church, and I am saved by membership." Another common saying among certain religions is, "There is no salvation outside my church." This is the grossest piece of presumption imaginable because exactly the opposite is true. There is no salvation inside *or* outside the church! Salvation is by grace through faith alone in the work of Christ on Calvary's cross. Salvation is not merited simply because one is in good standing with a local church fellowship. Indeed, we should assemble ourselves together in Christian fellowship, but we should never make the egregious assertion that salvation and church membership are the same thing. Because people are vulnerable to this doctrine, spiritual brokers have entered everywhere. When any local church becomes a spiritual broker, they have also become a synagogue of Satan.

Others make the claim that "my salvation is in my own personal goodness." While they do not claim to be perfectly righteous, they are conscious that they have not committed adultery, murder, or another terrible sin. They are generally good people. In this, many are to be commended, but all must realize that personal goodness has nothing to do with salvation. Salvation comes to us on the basis of imputed righteousness, not earned righteousness. That is, we are saved by righteousness which is put to our account rather than by righteousness that results from personal achievement. To be saved, our righteousness must exceed that of the scribes and the Pharisees, and only imputed righteousness can do that. The Lord Himself, when explaining salvation to the masses, declared, "Many will say to Me on that day, 'Lord, Lord, did we not prophesy in Your name, and in Your name cast out demons, and in Your name perform many miracles?' And then I will declare to them, 'I never knew you; depart from Me, you who practice lawlessness'" (Matthew 7:22,23).

There are those, of course, who claim, "I am going to heaven because I've spent my life helping others." Helping others is certainly commendable but alas, apart from faith in Christ, it is of no value whatsoever. First Corinthians 13:3, which speaks beautifully to the issue of love, also notes, "If I give all my possessions to feed the poor, and if I deliver my body to be burned, but do not have love, it profits me nothing." We are saved by grace alone.

Not long ago I was asked, "But doesn't the teaching of the grace of God produce wayward lives on the part of those who believe this?" The answer is simple: Nothing could be further from the truth. The Bible declares, "For the grace of God has appeared, bringing salvation to all men, instructing us to deny ungodliness and worldly desires and to live sensibly, righteously and godly in the present age, looking for the blessed hope and the appearing of the glory of our great God and Savior, Christ Jesus" (Titus 2:11-13). The first mark of a great church or institution is the preaching of the gospel of salvation by grace. All other points of emphasis, when speaking of salvation, are not Christian but cultic. Regularly, then, the church should sing,

Marvelous grace of our loving Lord,
Grace that exceeds our sin and our guilt.
Yonder on Calvary's mount outpoured,
There where the blood of the Lamb was spilt.
Grace, grace, God's grace, grace that will
pardon and cleanse within.
Grace, grace, God's grace, grace that is greater
than all our sin.

Let no cultic promoter tell you differently. *Salvation is by grace alone.* It is very dangerous for anyone to have a false basis for salvation. Such a person faces the danger of a wasted life and a lost eternity. Remember that the Philippian jailer asked the apostle Paul, "What must I do to be saved?" In response, Paul did not answer the question. Rather, he answered as if the jailer had asked, "What must I believe to be saved?" Then Paul's answer was clearly given: "Believe on the Lord Jesus Christ, and you shall be saved" (Acts 16:31). We are not saved by what we *do* but by what we *believe*.

Study Questions

1. How did you come to know the Lord Jesus Christ as your personal Savior?

2. What is the basis of your salvation? How do you know you are truly saved?

3. How does your assurance of salvation differ from a cult member who is working toward his salvation?

4. How is the law a "curse," according to Galatians 3:10,11?

5. What does it mean to be declared righteous, and what implication does that have for your spiritual life?

An Uncertain Hope

The soul that is in distress is also in bondage!

If a person's distress can be perpetuated by a religious promoter, that promoter can be reasonably sure of keeping the distressed soul in continuing and ever-increasing bondage. The religious charlatan must be very careful never to produce a final cure. Instead, he must push certainty up into an unrealizable future in order to keep needy souls striving toward the goal. Therefore, we ought not be surprised that an almost universal characteristic of the cults in our time is their insistence that one can never be sure of eternal life while in this world. The issue of salvation is never settled. The follower lives in constant fear that he has not done enough, given enough, prayed enough, said enough, or worshiped enough to be sure of salvation. I suspect that the cults are really not talking about salvation at all, but are pushing religious philosophies tied to a set of unrealizable goals. Their aim is to extract every kind of sacrifice from their hapless followers.

Atheist Robert Ingersoll came close to describing leadership in programs like these cults when he said, "A preacher is one who is willing to take care of your affairs in the next world, providing you will support him in this one." That is a cynical but apt description of the false religious leader who is not really interested in producing the assurance of salvation. He would be out of business very quickly if he set people free. His support would cease. Cult promoters, being interested only in the fulfillment of their lust for power, money, or satisfaction, are very careful to extract from their followers a response today in return for a promise that can only be fulfilled tomorrow. Uncertainty is a favorite cult weapon. It would hardly be possible to promote a successful cult if one offered the assurance of salvation or any sure hope of eternal life based upon the finished work of another.

Certain Salvation

The New Testament gospel is in contrast to all of this. The Bible promises the believing Christian that he is the possessor of certain salvation: "Blessed be the God and Father of our Lord Jesus Christ, who according to His great mercy has caused us to be born again to a living hope through the resurrection of Jesus Christ from the dead, to obtain an inheritance which is imperishable and undefiled and will not fade away, reserved in heaven for you, who are protected by the power of God through faith for a salvation ready to be revealed in the last time. In this you greatly rejoice" (1 Peter 1:3-6).

The Bible promises that the believer is "sealed with that Holy Spirit of promise" (Ephesians 1:13). The Christian is the possessor of hope, both sure and steadfast (Hebrews 6:19). The cultists make no such promise. Because they are interested in producing perpetual obligation as opposed to spiritual freedom, they keep their followers in the hopeless bondage of a constant, insecure relationship with God. For the member of the cult there is always more to do or more to pay, and his hope of blessing in eternal life is a will-o'-the-wisp that can never be realized in this life. A hope so uncertain is hardly a hope at all.

The Jehovah's Witnesses promise the new birth to only their inner 144,000. No one knows quite who constitutes this inner group or what will be the destiny of those outside of it. The followers of Theosophy are pursuing a set of philosophies so abstract that they produce no assurance at all. Edgar Cayce promised assurance only in some future life, saying, "Since we all have sinned and come short of the glory of God, we would be doomed if we only had one *Me* for making ourselves acceptable for the Father."

Pursuers in the inner-peace movement risk despair on the days in which their inner peace is less "real" to them than before. The Krishna crowd pursues a relativistic emergence into divinity in which no one can be certain where he stands at any given moment. They promise that if you live a life of Krishna consciousness then, when you leave your body, if you think of him you will achieve bliss. A thoughtful person who carefully examines the preaching and writing of the cults he's involved in is almost certain to sense a frustrating indefiniteness. He is being strung along, beguiled up a primrose path to nowhere.

It would be unthinkable for cults to ever embrace these words of Scripture: "For I am convinced that neither death, nor life, nor angels, nor principalities, nor things present, nor things to come, nor powers, nor height, nor depth, nor any other created thing, shall be able to separate us from the love of God, which is in Christ Jesus our Lord" (Romans 8:38,39).

What a blessed contrast we have in the encouraging words of the apostle Paul, "I know whom I have believed and I am convinced that He is able to guard what I have entrusted to Him until that day" (2 Timothy 1:12). Paul's absolute certainty of eternal life is revealed in the many statements of confidence he expressed:

For we know that if the earthly tent which is our house is torn down, we have a building from God, a house not made with hands, eternal in the heavens (2 Corinthians 5:1).

But I am hard-pressed from both [directions], having the desire to depart and be with Christ, for [that] is very much better (Philippians 1:23).

For our citizenship is in heaven, from which also we eagerly wait for a Savior, the Lord Jesus Christ; who will transform the body of our humble state into conformity with the body of His glory, by the exertion of the power that He has even to subject all things to Himself (Philippians 3:20,21).

For He delivered us from the domain of darkness, and transferred us to the kingdom of His beloved Son, in whom we have redemption, the forgiveness of sins (Colossians 1:13,14).

For you have died and your life is hidden with Christ in God. When Christ, who is our life, is revealed, then you also will be revealed with Him in glory (Colossians 3:3,4).

Then we who are alive and remain shall be caught up together with them in the clouds to meet the Lord in the air, and thus we shall always be with the Lord (1 Thessalonians 4:17).

The Bible celebrates our secure hope in God. Unlike the obscure future that is the best a cult can offer, Paul brightly tells us that Christ has "abolished death, and brought life and immortality to light through the gospel" (2 Timothy 1:10).

Trafficking in Uncertainty

We may be very sure that the promoter of a false religion, who is interested in producing dependence upon himself, would never pass on to his followers these words of Christ: "My sheep hear My voice, and I know them, and they follow Me; and I give eternal life to them, and they shall never perish; and no one shall snatch them out of My hand. My Father, who has given them to Me, is greater than all; and no one is able to snatch them out of the Father's hand" (John 10:27-29).

It is interesting to note that the verse immediately following this promise says, "Then the Jews took up stones again to stone Him." Natural man, even in the realm of religious leadership, will do anything to destroy the perfect confidence that a relationship with Jesus Christ brings to a life. The reason is very clear: *They traffic in uncertainty.*

The person who is anxious is also exploitable. To make him fearful is the design of these religious leaders; they use fear to create dependence upon the religious view they are promoting. Cult gathering places are populated by frightened people who live in terror of falling into the disfavor of their religious establishment. Our modern society is not without many tragic wrecks of humanity whose psychic natures have been shattered and their confidence destroyed as a result of previous involvement in false religions. To these people we happily repeat the wonderful promise: "If therefore the Son shall make you free, you shall be free indeed" (John 8:36).

Christians have always taken great confidence in that marvelous statement of faith given to us by the patriarch Job. He, as you will remember, lost everything. The time came when this destitute servant of God was at the end of himself. He had no great theological argument with which to analyze his condition. Nevertheless, from the bottom of the pit of spiritual desolation, he stated one of the great affirmations of faith: "As for me, I know that my Redeemer lives, and at the last He will take His stand on the earth.

Even after my skin is destroyed, yet from my flesh I shall see God" (Job 19:25,26). In his condition, Job could not have argued for a prosperity gospel or another of the "modern versions" of Christianity existing today. It was only through his faith that he knew his present and future were in the hands of God. Talk about security—Job had it!

The believing Christian has a hundred blessings going for him in the days of his earthly sojourn. These will not change when he departs this veil of tears and is transported into the arms of Jesus. We who believe the gospel should think of this every day and rejoice in it every night. We should also remember to reach out to those caught in religious circumstances that deny the solidity of their faith through time and into eternity. We need to share the message that eternal life is a free gift, and it has a certain outcome: a home in heaven in the presence of Jesus Christ. The cult organizer who preaches a different message is doing so for his own personal aggrandizement. What he says about an uncertain salvation is not the teaching of Scripture, but rather the emanations of his own evil, promotional mind.

It is unthinkable, says the pseudo-intellectual, that God should give such a gift as eternal life and give it away for nothing. We agree and that is what makes the gospel so amazing. The doctrine of *quid pro quo* reigns in this world in all human transactions. This doctrine is not applicable to the gift of salvation. God requires nothing in return on our part, save faith in the finished work of Christ on the cross. We Christians mean it when we sing "Calvary covers it all." Anything short of this *is not* true Christianity.

STUDY QUESTIONS

1. In what does a Christian place his hope?

2. What joyful promise does 1 Peter 1:3-6 give you regarding your hope?

3. How is the Holy Spirit the guarantor of hope, according to Ephesians 1:11-14?

4. How does keeping followers unsure of their hope work to a cult leader's advantage?

5. How evident is Paul's hope in 2 Timothy 1:8-12?

Meet Your New Leader

Only Jesus Christ deserves disciples!

This towering fact is ignored by most of the religions in the world today. The Christian message is that Jesus Christ is the author and finisher of our faith (Hebrews 12:2). He alone is our high priest (Hebrews 4:14). He alone is our mediator (1 Timothy 2:5). He is the head of the church, the body of Christ (Ephesians 1:22,23).

To the Christian, Jesus Christ is all in all (Colossians 3:11). We have a telling example of this in that gracious individual whom God called to be a forerunner of Jesus Christ, John the Baptist. Because of his remarkable ministry, John became the object of great spiritual interest. This spiritual interest produced a tremendous following. Many potential followers of John asked questions that implied they wanted to attribute to him some divine qualities and make him their leader. What was the Baptist's answer? The apostle John gives us the most fascinating account:

> And this is the witness of John, when the Jews sent to him priests and Levites from Jerusalem to ask him, "Who are you?" And he confessed, and did not deny, and he confessed, "I am not the Christ."
>
> And they asked him, "What then? Are you Elijah?"
>
> And he said, "I am not."
>
> "Are you the Prophet?"

And he answered, "No."

They said then to him, "Who are you, so that we may give an answer to those who sent us? What do you say about yourself?"

He said, "I am a voice of one crying in the wilderness, 'Make straight the way of the Lord,' as Isaiah the prophet said." (John 1:19-23).

When asked these questions, John the Baptist may well have been tempted to at least be a bit mysterious about his true nature. How delightful is his instant, honest response, "I am not the Christ." While others might have been tempted to grab some of the glory for themselves, John would have none of it. "No, no, no" was the form of his emphatic denial of any messianic quality. He insisted on exalting Jesus Christ, saying, "This was He of whom I said, 'He who comes after me has a higher rank than I, for He existed before me'" (John 1:15).

Presumptuous Messianic Leadership

John the Baptist left us a most commendable example by constantly deferring to God the praise and applause of the humanity gathered about him. Later, there were those who came to inform John that "all men" were coming and following Jesus Christ. John's answer is the essence of humility: "A man can receive nothing, unless it has been given him from heaven. You yourselves bear me witness, that I said, 'I am not the Christ,' but, 'I have been sent before Him.' He who has the bride is the bridegroom; but the friend of the bridegroom, who stands and hears him, rejoices greatly because of the bridegroom's voice. And so this joy of mine has been made full. He must increase, but I must decrease" (John 3:27-30).

How fearful is the contrast between John the Baptist and the life and ministry of many religious leaders in our time. The cults are replete with leaders who state or imply they have some unusual divine capability that should inspire worship on the part of their followers. In 1954, Sun Myung Moon founded the "Holy Spirit Association for the Unification of World Christianity." This Korean millionaire and religious promoter claims hundreds of thousands of followers worldwide, and he fosters in them the belief that he is the "Lord of the Second Advent," the personalized second coming of Jesus Christ. Moon rose out of his Presbyterian and Pentecostal background to organize a cult around a new theology that presents him as the great hope for mankind. He and his second wife are put forth as the new Adam and Eve, and their followers are the first children of a new and perfect world.

Judge Rutherford of the Jehovah's Witnesses likewise presented himself as "God's chosen vessel" and the Watchtower organization as the final dispenser of truth. Joseph Smith of the Mormons claimed that John the Baptist had given him the priesthood of Aaron. As if this were not enough, he later claimed that he had received a higher priesthood, that of Melchizedek, directly from Peter, James, and John. His followers repeatedly claim that he has done more for the salvation of this world than any other man who has ever lived, except Jesus. The late L. Ron Hubbard of the Scientology cult offered himself as a higher authority than Jesus Christ or the Christian Bible. This science fiction writer produced a devoted set of followers who pressed millions of dollars into his hands and his organization.

In the same way, Guru Maharaj Ji has presented himself as the "perfect master" and the "lord of the universe" and is esteemed as such by his thousands of followers across America and the world. It is ironic that this exalted personality, being a juvenile, had to get permission from a local judge to marry his 24-year-old secretary. And Meher Baba of the Baha'i cult has said, "There is no doubt of my being God personified. . . . I am the Christ. . . . I assert unequivocally that I AM infinite consciousness; I make this assertion because I AM infinite consciousness. I am everything and I am beyond everything. . . . Before me was Zoroaster, Krishna, Rama, Buddha, Jesus, and Mohammed. . . . My present avataric form is the last incarnation of the cycle of time, hence my manifestation will be the greatest."

All of these religious carpetbaggers have presumed for themselves the role of messianic leader.

The Final Authority

One of the marks of a cult is that it elevates the person and the words of a human leader to a messianic level. The predictable characteristic of a cult member is that he will soon be quoting his leader, whether Father Divine, Prophet Jones, Mary Baker Eddy, Judge Rutherford, Herbert Armstrong, or Buddha as the final authority. An exalted human leader has used the powers of his intelligence or personality to impose his ideas and directives on the unsuspecting. The success of this approach is usually predictable, for too many religiously disposed people are not intellectually responsible enough to seriously question the claims. Their easy mental acquiescence has led them to seek a leader who can give them all of the answers and personalize or objectify their religious needs. They want someone to speak to them with authority, even finality. All too often converts to a religion stand in inordinate awe of the person who brought them into that faith.

Many religious persuaders have given into the temptation to personally promote themselves and retain their exalted image in the minds of their devoted followers. The temptation to change from a simple servant to an exalted messiah can be very strong in the life of a charismatic leader. It is possible that many cult organizers began as humble people who came to believe their own promotions. They soon stamp their names on everything and push themselves as being utterly indispensable to the faith of their followers. They often cleverly continue to promote the image of external humility while in fact spending millions to keep their names in lights before their starry-eyed followers. "My people need me," is their assumption, "and bless them, they can have me—for a price."

No Christian should make such a mistake. He is aware that all have sinned and come short of the glory of God. He knows that from the least to the greatest each Christian, but for the grace, the *unmerited* favor of Jesus Christ, would be corrupt and lost. He remembers what one apostle said: "By the grace of God I am what I am" (1 Corinthians 15:10).

The Christian has no final human leader except Jesus Christ. He is warned about this by Christ, who said, "But do not be called Rabbi; for One is your Teacher, and you are all brothers. And do not call anyone on earth your father; for One is your Father, He who is in heaven. And do not be called leaders; for One is your Leader, that is, Christ. But the greatest among you shall be your servant" (Matthew 23:8-11). The followers of Christ are not masters of one another; they relate to one another as members of a body. They are to serve one another (see Galatians 5:13). They are to submit themselves to one another (see 1 Corinthians 16:16). The Scriptures declare that when believers announce themselves as devoted followers of a human leader, they have sunk into carnality: "For you are still fleshly. For since there is jealousy and strife among you, are you not fleshly, and are you not walking like mere men? For when one says, 'I am of Paul,' and another, 'I am of

Apollos,' are you not mere men?" (1 Corinthians 3:3,4). Even Paul, when writing to Timothy, humbly said to "consider what I say, for the Lord will give you understanding in everything" (2 Timothy 2:7).

Any person who professes to be a true Christian makes a mistake when he calls himself by the name of any human leader. Scripture sternly reminds us, "You were bought with a price; do not become slaves of men" (1 Corinthians 7:23). It is the duty of a Christian to glorify God and to exercise great discretion in giving honor to men and women.

Servants of God

Few of us will meet more than two or three truly great people in the whole of our lifetimes. Notice how many "great" men of the Old Testament had but a brief era of greatness, then died fools. The stories of Samson, David, Solomon, and many other great men of biblical and religious history are simply the stories of *humanity* in its truest form. Those who are born of the flesh are flesh, and no mysterious self-deification will ever make that change.

The religious leader in our time must take great care in this regard. He must sternly prevent admirers from becoming enamored of his leadership rather than the leadership of Jesus Christ. In this he is doing no more than following the example of our Lord, who "emptied Himself, taking the form of a bond-servant, and being made in the likeness of men. And being found in appearance as a man, He humbled Himself by becoming obedient to the point of death, even death on a cross" (Philippians 2:7,8). This same Lord Jesus warned us that "he who speaks from himself seeks his own glory" (John 7:18). Christ spoke most critically of the chief religious leaders of His day because they "loved the approval of men rather than the approval of God" (John 12:43).

One who would aspire to be an effective servant of Jesus Christ must never forget that the servant is not greater than his lord. The messenger is not greater than the one who sent the message (John 13:16,17). The person who seeks glory from a human following does well to remember the fickleness of the crowd. Paul finally had to write to his constituents at Galatia and ask, "Have I therefore become your enemy by telling you the truth?" (Galatians 4:16). Jesus Christ warned us along those same lines, saying, "Woe to you when all men speak well of you, for in the same way their fathers used to treat the false prophets" (Luke 6:26). He expanded on this theme, noting, "Blessed are you when men cast insults at you, and persecute you, and say all kinds of evil against you falsely, on account of Me" (Matthew 5:11). It is clear, then, that the credential of a true servant of Jesus Christ is not the applause of the multitudes.

Special Prayer Abilities?

Another form of presumptuous messianic leadership in the religious scene is the claim some leaders make regarding their own abilities as special intercessors with God. Their followers are asked by them to "believe in my prayers" and to "give me the opportunity to pray for you." There is a general promotional build-up that asserts that the leader, because of his special gifts or deep spirituality, has some unusual powers with which to gain leverage before the throne of God. The claim to special prayer ability by the spiritual leader is a cruel device that has beguiled into servitude millions of sheeplike followers. Then these followers have been exploited to a frightening degree. This shameful doctrine of special access to God is false and foreign to the teachings of the New Testament.

By contrast to the heretical view of "special prayer ability," Jesus spoke to every believer, saying, "Whatever you ask in My name, that will I do, that the Father may be glorified in the Son" (John 14:13). Protestant Christianity was built on the sound biblical doctrine of the priesthood of every believer. The clear teaching of the New Testament is that *each* person who has been justified by faith in Jesus Christ has access to the Father in prayer. The Christian needs no human mediator. The doctrine of the priesthood of every believer needs to be rediscovered and reemphasized in the Christian sphere today. Without this emphasis on sound doctrine, the messianic tendency on the part of leaders to claim special favor with God will produce a new, deadly religious hierarchy.

No one has an inside track with God except Jesus Christ! No one has any access at all to the Father without Jesus Christ, and in Him we *all* are freely welcomed to the throne of grace. One of the great promises of the Bible to every believer is found in Paul's words to Timothy: "For there is one God, and one mediator between God and men, the man Christ Jesus" (1 Timothy 2:5). Similarly, the promise of the writer of the book of Hebrews is a blessed source of confidence to every child of God: "Since then we have a great high priest who has passed through the heavens, Jesus the Son of God, let us hold fast our confession. For we do not have a high priest who cannot sympathize with our weaknesses, but One who has been tempted in all things as we are, yet without sin. Let us therefore draw near with confidence to the throne of grace, that we may receive mercy and may find grace to help in time of need" (Hebrews 4:14-16).

Every believer in Jesus Christ is a priest and has access to the Father because of the work of our great high priest, Jesus Christ. The writer of Hebrews went on to encourage all believers by saying, "Since therefore, brethren, we have confidence to enter the holy place by the blood of Jesus, by a new and living way which He inaugurated for us through the veil, that is, His flesh, and since we have a great priest over the house of God, let us draw near with a sincere heart in full assurance of faith, having our hearts sprinkled clean from an evil conscience and our bodies washed with pure water" (Hebrews 10:19-22).

The believer who responds to this blessed invitation of Scripture will never again be subject to the presumptuous messianic leadership of someone who arrogantly claims a special prayer relationship with God. In time of trouble, the believer will no longer call some "prayer team" in a distant city, but will move by a new and living way into the holy place with the Lord Himself. Should the Christian desire also the prayers of others, he can meet before the throne of grace with his humble friends. Distant hands laid on stacks of letters are nothing compared to present believers meeting in prayer with Jesus Christ before the throne of God.

A Personal Relationship

When Paul prayed for believers, he prayed that they would know the personal access they had to God and the wonderful powers that were available to them by virtue of their personal relationship to the Lord:

> For this reason I too, having heard of the faith in the Lord Jesus which exists among you, and your love for all the saints, do not cease giving thanks for you, while making mention of you in my prayers; that the God of our Lord Jesus Christ, the Father of glory, may give to you a spirit of wisdom and of revelation in the knowledge of Him. I pray that the eyes of your heart may be enlightened, so that you may know what is the hope of His calling, what are the riches of the glory of His inheritance in the

saints, and what is the surpassing greatness of His power toward us who believe. These are in accordance with the working of the strength of His might. (Ephesians 1:15-19).

Later in the same epistle, Paul continues to pray that each of us "may be able to comprehend with all the saints what is the breadth and length and height and depth, and to know the love of Christ which surpasses knowledge, that you may be filled up to all the fulness of God" (Ephesians 3:18,19). Who can escape noticing the humility and tender spiritual concern in the apostle Paul as he labored to bring each individual believer to Christian maturity, into the full realization of the privileges that were his from the Lord? Surely one of the great needs in the church is a restatement and understanding of the individual destiny of the believer. The great relationship for the Christian is that personal one he has between himself and his Lord. This relationship continues, made viable by the Holy Spirit who, independent of any human mediator, lives within the heart of every believer.

In true Christianity no priest, no witchdoctor, no counselor, and no human intercessor is necessary between the heart of the believer and the heart of God. The Scripture instructs every believer to let his or her requests be made known unto God, for the Lord *desires* us to pray to Him. Every believer is invited to develop a growing personal relationship with the Lord. The message of the New Testament is very clear: The course in the life of the believer must move from dependence on the leadership of humans to independence of that leadership in the direction of a growing personal relationship with the Lord.

In the cult scene today, cult leaders labor to produce idolatrous dependence upon themselves. The mark of the cult leader is that he makes himself imperative in the lives of those who have become ensnared in his web. This tragic development is only made possible because of ignorance of the teaching in the Word of God on the part of many people. The message of Scripture is that the individual must not commit himself to allegedly infallible human leaders. Rather, he must become a follower of Jesus Christ, who alone is the head of the church.

When a human being made in the image of God becomes an other-oriented automaton in his religious life, he negates the purpose for which he was created. Divine cosmology is destroyed by religious concepts that produce servants of a human master instead of true followers of Jesus Christ. This satanic tendency was forever refuted by Jesus Christ when He said, "It is written, 'You shall worship the Lord your God and serve Him only'" (Luke 4:8).

The Repository of Truth

The cult leader also strengthens his presumptuous leadership by arrogating the position of being the only repository of divine truth. He frequently talks about "my message, my revelation, my leadership, my people." In doing this, he is pushing the heretical proposition that he has been made the true custodian of private revelations from God. Concerning this we have the clear teaching of the Word of God that no Scripture is of any private interpretation (see 2 Peter 1:20).

True religious leaders should emulate the apostle Paul, who was careful never to press his leadership to the place where he would control the lives of others. There are too few leaders in the world of religion who could say with him, "Not that we lord it over your faith, but are workers with you for your joy; for in your faith you are standing firm" (2 Corinthians 1:24). Paul was careful to remind each Christian that he himself possesses "wisdom, righteousness, sanctification, and redemption" in Jesus Christ. Beyond this, the believer, without the help of any guru, possesses everything else he needs. "The Lord knows the reasonings of the wise, that they are useless. So then let no one boast in men. For all things belong to you, whether Paul or Apollos or Cephas or the world or life or death or things present or things to come; all things belong to you, and you belong to Christ; and Christ belongs to God" (1 Corinthians 3:20-23).

The Bible is the repository of truth. Every individual believer possesses divine truth for himself when he holds the Word of God in his hand. The function of true Christian leadership is to bring each child of God to the point of maturity, where he can study the Bible for himself and be delivered from his dependence on a human teacher.

Only Jesus Christ deserves disciples. We can discover how serious this matter of false, presumptuous, and subversive spiritual leadership is by listening to the clear teachings of Scripture. Knowing that today's conditions would come to pass, the Holy Spirit spoke through the apostle Peter saying,

> But false prophets also arose among the people, just as there will also be false teachers among you, who will secretly introduce destructive heresies, even denying the Master who bought them, bringing swift destruction upon themselves. And many will follow their sensuality, and because of them the way of the truth will be maligned; and in their greed they will exploit you with false words; their judgment from long ago is not idle, and their destruction is not asleep (2 Peter 2:1-3).

Peter went on to describe the final outcome of the lives of such deceivers when he added,

> For if God did not spare angels when they sinned, but cast them into hell and committed them to pits

of darkness, reserved for judgment; and did not spare the ancient world, but preserved Noah, a preacher of righteousness, with seven others, when He brought a flood upon the world of the ungodly; and if He condemned the cities of Sodom and Gomorrah to destruction by reducing them to ashes, having made them an example to those who would live ungodly thereafter; and if He rescued righteous Lot, oppressed by the sensual conduct of unprincipled men (for by what he saw and heard that righteous man, while living among them, felt his righteous soul tormented day after day with their lawless deeds), then the Lord knows how to rescue the godly from temptation, and to keep the unrighteous under punishment for the day of judgment (2 Peter 2:4-9).

Finally, Peter calls the presumptuous and satanic leaders "unreasoning animals, born as creatures of instinct to be captured and killed, reviling where they have no knowledge, will in the destruction of those creatures also be destroyed" (2 Peter 2:12). Upon reading this passage of the Word of God, everyone should be sobered by the consequences of sin and fearful of this result taking place in any life. Scripture gives us an indication of the very depths of iniquity that live in the minds of hypocrites and spiritual pretenders. Notice that the church is warned about false teachers, but not about false prophets. Nowhere in the New Testament is the church warned of false prophets. Again and again it is warned about teachers and teachings. The implication is, as evangelical Bible teachers have contended, that prophets will not be a part of latter Christianity but teachers will. What does the Scripture say they will do? It tells us they will be purveyors of secret and damnable heresies. It says also that many shall follow their pernicious ways. It reminds us that they, with feigned words, will make merchandise of many. Scripture tells us also that they will have eyes full of adultery, and they will be unstable souls, practicing covetousness and cursing. The implication is that down the street from where some of us live could be a thriving, murderous cult. One young man in a cult in Mississippi recently killed a girlfriend, his mother, and several school friends. Another in southern California promised that his followers, if they followed him in suicide, would go through heaven's gate to a better world. Strange insanities set in the minds of people when wicked leadership becomes messianic and murderous. Second Peter 2 in the Word of God should cause *every* serious Christian to be careful, prayerful, and rightfully concerned about secret cultic activity.

STUDY QUESTIONS

1. What titles are given to Jesus in Scripture?

2. In our own day, where do you see religious leaders presuming messianic leadership for themselves?

3. What clear teaching did Jesus give us in Matthew 23:8-11?

4. What would you say to someone who claimed his or her religious leader had a miraculous ability to get prayers answered?

5. According to John 12:42,43, why do some people choose to claim a special relationship with God, even though they know it isn't true?

What Do We Believe?

If the trumpet give an uncertain sound, who shall prepare himself for the battle?

The answer to this biblical question is that many strange people will. Multitudes seem ready to answer an uncertain sound. Response may come from masses of individuals as they move out from the dark haunts of personal failure and confusion. There are increasing numbers of people living in our generation to whom uncertain sounds seem to be beautiful music. To them uncertainty is a form of certainty, and ambiguity satisfies the mind more than anything specific.

It is no wonder that these types are attracted to the constantly changing doctrines of cult religions. Doctrinal ambiguity is a mark of a cult. One of the fascinating characteristics of the cults is the interesting and sometimes hilarious changes of doctrine through which they pass. Their doctrines are being continually altered in order to adapt themselves to new situations, arguments, or the whims of their leaders. They know nothing of the command of Scripture that we "no longer be children, tossed here and there by waves, and carried about by every wind of doctrine, by the trickery of men, by craftiness in deceitful scheming" (Ephesians 4:14). The Bible is clear that craftily changing doctrine is a cunning device used by those who prey upon the unwary.

The illustrations are many. During and after the days of Mary Baker Eddy, the Christian Science cult republished her book *Science and Health with Key to the Scriptures* nearly every year. The annual update made it possible for the glaring contradictions and preposterous doctrines of the past to be adapted to the new demands of the present.

Guru Maharaj Ji says,

> Are you feeling thirsty? Can you see that photo of Lord Shiva? You see the water coming out from the top of his head? Drink that water. Drink, drink! Can you? You can't drink that water. It is a picture. You need everything living. If you have doubts, you cannot ask Lord Krishna questions. That's why you need a living Master, for the circumstances of the world today. When Jesus was here there were no nuclear bombs. But now there are nuclear bombs, and the Perfect Master, the Perfect Savior, has come to save you from nuclear bombs.

This strange religious leader who gained prominence at the age of 16 in the United States was once asked the question, "What part does mantra play in meditation?" His clear, precise answer was,

> Nothing, nothing. It just makes your tongue in gears, that's all. Makes your mind flicker into some other way, that's all. But mind is still flickering. When I say "Ram, Rrrr-Aaaa-Ma" three times my mind flickers in one word: "Ram." More flickering of your mind—no good, no help. That is the question I place before people: "You say Ram today, but what were the people saying before Ram was born?" Chanting is an external thing. See?

Of course, we don't see. There is simply no way the rational mind can make any sense out of these expressions. They have no meaning, and the Guru himself offers no answer because he isn't sure what he believes. There is no logical, organized system of beliefs in his cult, merely ponderous, confused pronouncements. In a word, what he lacks is called *doctrine*.

The word *doctrine* has no meaning in the fever swamps of the mind, which are inhabited by the cults, for doctrine means a systematic presentation and understanding of truth. The idea of doctrine is virtually unique to organized Christianity. We know exactly what we believe, for the truth of the faith has been plainly laid out in Scripture. By contrast, what passes for doctrine in a cult is really a subrational set of disconnected thoughts and practices that only serve to confuse the mind and the emotions. God gave us emotions so they might be the source of exhilaration, happiness, and joy at the understanding of truth and the end of duty. Emotions were never intended to be an end in themselves, and they are totally untrustworthy as the custodians of truth. Any religion that deliberately bypasses rational doctrinal understanding and seeks to build upon the emotions will inevitably deceive rather than enlighten.

From Sound Doctrine to Spiritual Abstractions

The use of chants, the clanging of cymbals, the singsong repetition of simple musical structures, the repeated staccato articulation of any word that is supposed to represent God, joy, or peace—all of these practices are subrational. They are calculated to play on the limited strings of the emotional structure, creating what passes as a religious experience but is actually nothing more than a mindless emotional trauma. Christ declared in Matthew 6 that we are not heard because of our "meaningless repetition." This is a statement that is regularly ignored by the cults.

The Krishna devotees are big on chanting, holding that their tuneless incantations are the way to all knowledge and the key to salvation. Their own literature explains:

> The chanting of the *maha-mantra*—Hare Krishna, Hare Krishna, Krishna Krishna, Hare—is the recommended chant of this age. *Man* means "mind," and *tra* means "deliverance." Therefore, a *mantra* is a chant meant to deliver the mind from all unwanted thoughts. *Maha* means "great." The Hare Krishna *maha-mantra* is the great chanting to deliver the mind from all unwanted thoughts which keep us from realizing our true selves. Our consciousness is originally pure or *Krishna* consciousness, but now, due to association with material nature, our minds are filled with impure thoughts.[4]

This set of spiritual abstractions, resembling the Hinduism that has already brought poverty and despair to millions in India, is now being preached in the United States. The initial chief purveyor was "His Divine Grace A.C. Bhaktivedanta Swami Prabhupada," who is the spiritual master of the International Society for Krishna Consciousness. His magazine *Back to Godhead* explains about Prabhupada, saying,

> He has mercifully given the chanting of Hare Krishna to the world so that everyone may regain his original joyful consciousness and live in peace and happiness. By chanting these holy names, we reestablish our lost link with the Supreme and enjoy our real life, which is fun of eternity, knowledge, and bliss. Srila Prabhupada has asked, "Please chant these holy names of the Lord. Your life will become sublime."

Apparently just by endlessly repeating these words some sort of abstract magic is supposed to change our lives and bring us joy. Exactly how this happens isn't clear, but the emotional charge offered by the cult wipes away most concerns for logic in the minds of followers.

The illustrations of doctrinal ambiguity from the old and the new cults are endless. Never in the history of the world have there been so many confused and contradictory religious propositions pressed upon people in the guise of truth. The mind reels in confusion at any attempt to understand with any logical comprehension the preaching and doctrinal system of modern-day cults.

Avoiding Ambiguity

This mindlessness of the cults is a most useful device. The cult promoters are not truly appealing to the mind, but rather are attempting to set the mind aside in order to appeal to a set of religious emotions. Devotees say to one another in effect, "Forget what he is saying, can't you *feel* the vibrations? Surely we are in divine presence as the guru is speaking to us." Logic and order take a backseat to emotion and ambiguity.

The "divine presence" is always justified by calling it "higher knowledge," "deeper truth," or some other adjective that excuses it from being the real thing. Converts are not urged to *understand*; rather, it is recommended that they *feel*. Terms like "self-realization," along with vague concepts about love, peace, and joy, are the expressions in which they traffic. The words of the cults are the products of a corrupted language. The words themselves have no real meaning—they have become emotional triggers connoting whatever you want them to mean. The cult promoters have denied the doctrine of objective value as relates to the words they use.

By contrast, our Lord Jesus Christ was very careful about the use of His words. The result is that those who heard went away saying that they had "never heard anyone who spoke like this man spoke." Christ clearly warned us of the utter importance of the proper use of words with real meaning, saying, "For by your words you shall be justified, and by your words you shall be condemned" (Matthew 12:37). The Word of God is very careful to avoid ambiguity. The contrast between bewildering, ever-changing cult doctrines and true Christianity is a very marked one. Nothing is clearer than Scripture's call to sound doctrine. The words of the New Testament lend themselves to a careful exposition of the truth of God.

Indeed, unlike the religions of the world, Christianity commits itself to careful details of all kinds. The Bible is filled with notations of cities, villages, rivers, dates, times, kings, and exact quotes of what many individuals have said. Like no book in all of the world, the Bible is a book of careful historic detail. In addition to this, important theological propositions are stated in many ways so there won't be any question about the meaning. So clear and broad is the presentation of the facts of the gospel that Paul was able to say to Timothy, "But you followed my teaching [literally *doctrine*], conduct, purpose, faith, patience, love, perseverance" (2 Timothy 3:10). We see then that clarity of belief is one of the characteristics of true Christianity. That's why Jesus said, "I am the light of the world; he who follows Me shall not walk in the darkness, but shall have the light of life" (John 8:12).

Philosophy vs. Truth

The Christian who studies the Word of God becomes spiritually mature, a defender of the faith, and a teacher. The clear doctrines of Holy Scripture can be understood to the point of certainty by faithful people as they are transmitted from person to person, place to place, and age to age. Paul wrote to his young protégé, "The things which you have heard from me in the presence of many witnesses, these entrust to faithful men, who will be able to teach others also" (2 Timothy 2:2).

It is imperative that Christians know and teach the Word of God, for the Bible clearly warns that "the time will come when they will not endure sound doctrine; but wanting to have their ears tickled, they will accumulate for themselves teachers in accordance to their own desires; and will turn away their ears from the truth, and will turn aside to myths"(2 Timothy 4:3,4).

Fables, predicted in Scripture, are one of the marks of a cult. One can listen endlessly to cultic representatives on radio and television and never be sure what they are talking about. They pose questions which they do not answer, and they offer answers to unexplainable questions. One of the most mentally frustrating experiences in life is to attempt to decide exactly what a religious promoter meant by what he said. The answer cannot be found even by reading hundreds of pages of his literature. Instead, the reader is led into an ever deeper labyrinth of confusion. This is the way they plan it; they *intend* to confuse, not clarify. Being confused themselves, they are only able to throw dust in the air so that it gets in the eyes of others.

Consider some examples. It is almost impossible to understand what a Jehovah's Witness believes about God, biblical inspiration, eternity, and many other subjects. Armstrong's attempt to define the nature of the Godhead is a study in obfuscation—one finally concludes that we are to become a part of God, a frightening heresy indeed. And who can comprehend what the Inner Peace movement is really all about? The processions have given us a mass of impenetrable confusions in their new definitions of God, the devil, Christ, and the Holy Spirit. One almost suspects they put them all on the same level. Likewise the Unity people suggest that since God sees and understands perfectly, and sees no evil because there is no evil, we shall see clearly the unreality and futility of appearances of evil, to which, through a misunderstanding, man now attributes substance and reality. Soon they will deny the true humanity of humanity!

The tendency of the cults is to move away from the objective, categorical truth taught in Scripture in order to hide behind trees in the endless forest of philosophic discussion. To them the process of discussion is itself the truth. Nothing can be resolved because all things are continually and everlastingly relative. These indeed are people who are "always learning and never able to come to the knowledge of the truth" (2 Timothy 3:7).

Reflect for a moment on an illustration from the life of Christ concerning the difference between philosophic discussion and real truth. Christ was witnessing to the woman at the well. The real truth about herself was the last thing in the world the woman wanted to face. As a result, she attempted to push the discussion up into the realm of the philosophical, lest Christ get down to the case of her five husbands and her present adulterous life. One can almost hear her voice dripping with pseudo-sophistication as she says, "Sir, I perceive that You are a prophet. Our fathers worshiped in this mountain, and you people say that in Jerusalem is the place where men ought to worship."

But Jesus was having none of her philosophical posing. "Jesus said to her, 'Woman, believe Me, an hour is coming when neither in this mountain, nor in Jerusalem, shall you worship the Father. You worship that which you do not know; we worship that which we know, for salvation is from the Jews. But an hour is coming, and now is, when the true worshipers shall worship the Father in spirit and truth; for such people the Father seeks to be His worshipers" (John 4:19-23).

In most pointed fashion, Christ cut through the fog of meaningless verbiage and brought this woman face to face with reality. As with Nicodemus and many others, Christ would not allow the woman at the well to get away from the burning issue of her personal need, for it was a matter of life and death. She was soon rejoicing in the result because she believed in Christ and became an earnest witness to the reality of His salvation. So it is that the message of the gospel of Christ is continually presented in the Word as the profoundly beautiful and simple story of the Christ who died and rose again in order that we, by faith in Him, might have everlasting life.

By contrast, the dark night of doctrinal obscurity has settled on many segments of the current religious establishment because of the obfuscations and contradictions of the confused representatives of religions. The individual who seeks after truth in our time does well to heed the warning of Christ: "If anyone walks in the day, he does not stumble, because he sees the light of this world. But if anyone walks in the night, he stumbles, because the light is not in him" (John 11:9,10).

The great need in today's religious establishment is for the candid preaching of sound doctrine, not the tantalizing sentences of those who never quite get to the point. Thank God for the faithful Christian expositors of the Scriptures (may their tribe increase!) who can truthfully say, "I did not shrink from declaring to you anything that was profitable, and teaching you publicly and from house to house, solemnly testifying to both Jews and Greeks of repentance toward God and faith in our Lord Jesus Christ" (Acts 20:20,21).

Ambiguity is the devil's gospel, whereas clarity is divine. Given the importance of doctrine, we will definitely profit by a brief review of what sound doctrine truly is. It doesn't come from the person who speaks the loudest, has the most followers, or wears a funny hat. Doctrine, rather, is the biblical truth that makes Christianity Christianity. What do Christians truly believe constitutes the Christian faith? I believe the necessary doctrinal assertions include:

1. *The trinity:* Ours is the triune God, three persons in one, existing from eternity. We are not unitarians; we are trinitarians. The trinity consists of the Father, the Son, and the Holy Spirit, each of whom is coequal and coeternal with the others. Any religion that denies the trinity is satanic rather than divine. It is a cult.

2. *The verbal, plenary inspiration of the Bible:* We believe that "*all* Scripture is inspired by God and profitable for teaching, for reproof, for correction, for training in righteousness; that the man of God may be adequate, equipped for every good work" (2 Timothy 3:16,17). The Bible is the actual Word of God, by which we hear from Him.

3. *The deity of the Father, the Son, and the Holy Spirit:* The God who made the universe is, as the old hymn says, "God in three persons, blessed trinity." God is the Creator, the Almighty, the *only* divine being in existence.

4. *God became man in the person of the Son, Jesus Christ:* Christ is a unique individual in all of history. He is the God-man, entirely God and entirely man, consisting in one individual.

5. *The vicarious atonement of Christ:* On the cross, Christ died in our place, thereby putting away sin by the sacrifice of Himself. He died on our behalf as an act of love.

6. *The bodily resurrection:* Christ rose from the dead on the third day after His crucifixion, and He became the ever-living Lord. Without the resurrection, our faith is in vain.

7. *Man is a sinner:* Romans 3:23 tells us plainly that "all have sinned and come short of the glory of God." Man is therefore in need of a savior, for his sins separate him from God.

8. *Sinful man is justified by faith in Jesus Christ alone:* We are "justified as a gift by His grace through the redemption which is in Christ Jesus" (Romans 3:24). There is no other source of salvation.

9. *The believer is able to live to the glory of God:* By virtue of the indwelling Christ, our lives are changed. Whereas before we were spiritually dead to God, we are now alive in Christ Jesus.

10. *Christ is coming again in power and great glory:* One day soon the Lord will return "to judge the living and the dead" (2 Timothy 4:1). Every person will have to give an accounting of his life before God, and he will face eternity based upon his faith in the Lord Jesus.

Each of these is an undeniable truth from the Word of God. Not one of these propositions may be violated by anyone who claims to be a representative of the gospel of Christ. The cults, however, are famous for adding or subtracting to the gospel. They make it an instrument of deceit and error to those who hear. Instead of preaching truth, they replace it with philosophical sophistry.

The exact definition of the gospel is given to us in the Word of God: "Christ died for our sins according to the Scriptures. . . . He was buried, and . . . He was raised on the third day according to the Scriptures" (1 Corinthians 15:3,4).

Anything apart from this is not Christian and should be the object of our eternal opposition. Given this clear presentation of the gospel, one wonders why people are so prone to invent alternatives. The reasons could be anything from satanic motivation to personal aggrandizement.

Once the apostle Paul was waited upon by sophisticated "Christian" promoters from Jerusalem. They conferred with him about the necessity of keeping the law. Boldly, Paul describes this incident and says, "But we did not yield in subjection to them for even an hour, so that the truth of the gospel might remain with you" (Galatians 2:5). In similar fashion, we too must commit ourselves to the truth of the gospel and be willing to oppose every alternative, no matter what the cost. Many have defected from the truth of the gospel in our time. By so doing, they risk the possibility of dropping into the dreadful cults that have sprung up across the world. These naïve ones should be the focus of our prayers, so they will return to fidelity to Jesus Christ before it is too late. As one hymnwriter put it:

> *The soul that on Jesus hath leaned for repose,*
> *I will not, I will not desert to his foes;*
> *That soul, tho all hell should endeavor to shake,*
> *I'll never, no never, no never forsake!*

STUDY QUESTIONS

1. Why shouldn't you spend a lot of time studying the doctrines of a cult?

2. What is wrong with placing experience ahead of doctrine?

3. Why is the trinity an essential doctrine to the faith? Why is the inspiration of Scripture essential?

4. What instruction regarding doctrine does Paul give his protégé in 2 Timothy 2:2? What warning does he add in 4:3,4?

5. In 1 Corinthians 15:3,4, Paul summarized an essential doctrine of the faith. How would you summarize that truth?

Finding New Secrets

I have found the secret!

Few people are more fascinating than those who claim to have inside information on a given subject. Who of us as a child has not listened with breathless anticipation to stories of experiences told by older people? The sea, mountain caves, or the Khyber Pass lived for us in the tales that were passed on to us by those raconteurs. Stories of talking animals or mysterious haunted houses were a part of our youthful pursuits of fantasy.

Children's stories that are known to be fantasy are one thing; fantasies purveyed as religious truth are quite another. There is nothing wrong with listening to a storyteller and, after a smile or a tear, going on to do something else. The wrong, indeed the insane, course is to fall down at his feet and worship him. Fables that are known to be such are enjoyable little diversions in life. Religious fantasies that are presented as special spiritual discoveries are dangerous.

In every walk of life, from the world of investment to the world of religion, many have been conned out of their money, their eternal souls, or both by those who claim special knowledge from sources of information not commonly available. In this regard, the world of business is in many ways wiser than the world of religion. It is illegal for any person to purchase securities on the basis of "inside information," knowledge that isn't generally available to the average investor on the street. We could wish that in the world of religion there were such a law. Unfortunately, such a law would be impossible to pass. Even if it were enacted, it would be ignored by millions of people in pursuit of religious fascinations rather than truth.

The careful teacher of sound doctrine is rarely as electrifying as the mysterious religious promoter who, usually for a price, will let us in on his secret. Under the spells he casts we are often tempted to forget that the best things in life are not only free, but are usually obvious.

The Discovery of Secrets

The beauty of nature and the wonderful works of God are apparent to us on every hand. From an examination of these, we can discover our Lord's eternal power and Godhead (Romans 1:20). From a serious study of His Word, the Holy Bible, we have available to us everything in life, without exception. How wonderful is the promise of the Word of God! As the apostle Peter exulted, "Seeing that His divine power has granted to us everything pertaining to life and godliness, through the true knowledge of Him who called us by His own glory and excellence. For by these He has granted to us His precious and magnificent promises, in order that by them you might become partakers of the divine nature, having escaped the corruption that is in the world by lust" (2 Peter 1:3,4).

It is very clear that the humble Christian who will pursue the teachings of the Bible with simplicity and godly sincerity becomes the glad recipient of the abundant provision of God for every need for time and eternity. There can be no greater promise than that we are blessed "with all spiritual blessings in heavenly places in Christ" (Ephesians 1:3).

In the face of this open provision of all things freely given from God, one is amazed to see the large and loyal following that comes to people who report some vision, presence, revelation, or special discovery that has come to them, which they claim to be divine. It would be impossible to have a cult without mysterious, otherwise unavailable inside information. In one way or another, each of these dreadful religions traffics in such hallucinations.

The Christian must remember that there is no discovery in the entire universe that anyone could possibly have that is superior to his discovery of salvation in Jesus Christ. There is no higher information, no better revelation, no deeper truth—nothing is greater than the knowledge of Christ. The person who turns from this greatest discovery, this ultimate revelation, to pursue the delusions of a cult leader is a fool. Despite this obvious truth, the cults continue to beguile unstable souls with their false claims to special discoveries.

The British "Israelists" claim to have discovered the marvelous truth that the English people are the 10 lost tribes of Israel. They claim that the monarch of England actually sits on the throne of King David of Israel. She is his direct descendant and continues his dynasty, sitting also on the very throne on which Christ shall sit after His return to earth.

Misguided Americans and Englishmen, some of them famous, have traveled to India to learn of the special discoveries of some seedy guru who claims to have stumbled across the secrets of life. It is amazing that so many will seek such crumbs that fall from the table of a pagan religious philosopher when the very words of God are available to them on the pages of Holy Scripture.

The witchcraft cults in America prosper because of leaders who claim to have discovered the secret of prosperity, health, victory over our environment, or some other needed capability. People may flock into the train of the religious leader who has "discovered the secret" and seeks to pass it on to them.

Dag Thorleifsson of Iceland started a cult and encouraged followers to worship the old Viking gods. Another cult was born as a propagandist announced he had discovered old and long-hidden secrets which he was willing to make available. The Scientologists, who claim millions of followers in the city of Los Angeles alone, profess to have discovered that man has occupied a number of different bodies during his many incarnations in the world. They claim to be able to prove this by carrying an individual back along a "time track" to his earlier lifetimes to seek out the cause of his current problems.

The claim to special discoveries and repeatable-on-demand revelations from God is the point where the cults tend to move off into the occult. Witchcraft, spiritism, and Satan worship are nothing more than religions that assert they can call for the incursion of the metaphysical in the realm of the physical. This is surely one of the reasons why the cults are often but a stopping place where a disturbed soul lingers briefly before dropping totally into the pit of the occult. The Christian church has no secrets—the truth is proclaimed openly. When someone accepts Christ, they are not taken into a back room and shown a secret handshake or a secret code for interpreting Scripture. The Bible says that everything Jesus did was out in the open. So it is with His church. God has already given us His message through His Holy Word; there is no need for any additional revelation.

Nevertheless, the almost universal base of each cult is the purported revelation that one person received. These persons claim divine authority for a private, unauthenticated religious event. They claim to have seen a vision of a woman on a mountain, heard a voice in a prayer tower, or been visited by an angel who came with golden tablets and giant spectacles. The unsubstantiated and largely preposterous stories are endless.

The Response of Believers

What is the proper response to the claim of an individual to a new, divine discovery? His claim should be subjected to the biblical rules of evidence. The discovery may have been a hallucination, an outright lie, or even the result of indigestion or a sleepless night. How different is the truth of Christianity! It is not dependent upon claims by private individuals to special discoveries. *The fundamental characteristic of the faith of Christ is that it is based on historical fact.*

Talking of all of the events that centered around the life, work, death, and resurrection of Christ, the Scripture says that "this thing was not done in a corner" (Acts 26:26). Luke states that Christ declared Himself to be alive after His passion "by many infallible proofs" (Acts 1:3). There were hundreds, and in some cases thousands, of witnesses to the open and public facts of the gospel.

Often those to whom the gospel was preached were reminded that they knew of their own knowledge the truth of these things (Acts 26:25,26). The witnesses to the facts of the gospel were declared as being alive and responsible to testify of Christ (1 Corinthians 15:6). Nothing is more obvious in the writings of the Old and New Testaments than the fact of the public revelation and working of God in the presence of proofs and competent witnesses. The truth of Christianity does not depend on private knowledge or secret, unconfirmable relationships on the part of individuals.

Yet the growing activity of religious promoters with concocted stories should not come as a surprise to us. The
Scripture predicts:

> But false prophets also arose among the people,
> just as there will also be false teachers among you,
> who will secretly introduce destructive heresies,
> even denying the Master who bought them,
> bringing swift destruction upon themselves. And
> many will follow their sensuality, and because of
> them the way of the truth will be maligned; and in
> their greed they will exploit you with false words;
> their judgment from long ago is not idle, and their
> destruction is not asleep (2 Peter 2:1-3).

Notice that the heresies being brought in by false
teachers are *secret* and *destructive*. It would never be possible for these purveyors of their own imaginings to be successful were it not for the foolish inattention on the part of
many to the laws of evidence. Jesus Christ paid very careful
attention to these laws, saying, "If I bear witness of Myself,
My witness is not true" (John 5:31). Again and again Jesus
paid respect to the divine laws of evidence by naming those
other sources of data that would bear witness to the truth
of His Word: "I told you, and you do not believe; the works
that I do in My Father's name, these bear witness of Me"
(John 10:25).

Because of these abundant sources of evidence, the
apostle Peter was able to say, "We did not follow cleverly
devised tales when we made known to you the power and
coming of our Lord Jesus Christ, but we were eyewitnesses
of His majesty" (2 Peter 1:16). Nevertheless, the deceitful
infection of the cultic promoters continues as they beguile
unstable souls away from the clear and obvious truth and
into the unprovable mysteries they themselves cannot
explain.

The Secret Is Out!

The Christian who would be a good servant of the Lord does well to take the opposite course. The prophet Habakkuk gave us good advice in this regard, saying, "Then the LORD answered me and said, 'Record the vision and inscribe it on tablets, that the one who reads it may run'" (Habakkuk 2:2). The apostle Paul operated in similar fashion, saying, "We use great plainness of speech" (2 Corinthians 3:12).

It is a fair generalization to say that it is the duty of the true minister of the gospel to take the mysteries of God and make them plain. The normal direction of the cultic promoter is to take the plain truth of the Word and turn it into as mysterious a message as possible. Many deadly pitfalls lie along the path of the dark and the unknown. No Christian is required to believe that Jesus Christ has appeared to anyone since the day of the completion of Holy Scripture. God rests His case on the Bible. This Book should be plainly preached by those who stand in pulpits. It should be clearly taught by those who would expound truth. It should be carefully read by all who would discover the nature of reality. Then there will be no need for special discoveries on the part of anyone. The greatest discovery an individual can make is to experience the joy of a personal relationship with Jesus Christ, which comes by faith in His person and His work as revealed in Holy Scripture.

The secret is out! The gospel is available to all. Jesus Christ has come in the flesh and brought life and immortality to light through the gospel. Faith in Him brings a discovery that is special indeed—and available to all. Still, in opposition to the simplicity of the gospel, there are religious institutions, churches, and even museums which are filled with objects that are supposed to attest to a special revelation or unique, divine endowment. What does a person do who has no standing in any special sense with people? He invents a religion centered on himself and often produces an object to vouchsafe that mysterious acceptance. So it is that we have statues we revere, voices of "angels," strange incantations, occult communication with the past, and thousands of pieces of false proof that the present claimant to divine authority attempts to use as credentials. Many otherwise impotent usurpers of religious authority continue to try to influence others with their bogus claims to special discoveries. If their claims to one or another kind of authority are not the object of response, many times these cultic promoters become dangerous. Some of the leaders of cults have become embittered to the place of committing assaults and even murdering their recalcitrant followers. The flaming buildings which brought an end to the Koresh cult in Waco, Texas, may well be an illustration of this. Jesus spoke about the childishness of people whose claims to be somebody special were not motivating to people. "It is like children sitting in the market places," our Lord said, "who call out to the other children and say, 'We played the flute for you, and you did not dance; we sang a dirge, and you did not mourn'" (Matthew 11:16,17). How sad it is when unrequited cultic claims don't become the object of negative responses on the part of cynical hearers who, as the cult leaders often say, "are too childish to understand."

Still the promoters of absurd messages continue to proliferate in our world. They can be counted on to invent whatever source of artificial authority may be workable at the time. Carrying a statue of Christ, an image of the virgin, a message from the "queen of heaven," or whatever it may be, the cults continue to invent reality as they go along, "bringing swift destruction upon themselves," according to Peter. What's worse, "many will follow their sensuality" (2 Peter 2:1).

We must remind ourselves again that the truth of the gospel depends on the great event, the resurrection of Jesus Christ. From that point on, the gospel is a message to be preached, a story to tell to the nations. The attendant blessing of the Holy Spirit of God attests to the truth of that message. No other special revelatory miracles will be needed. The purveyors of such bogus magic are liars. Happy is the person who is delivered from such foolishness. Conversely, sad is the heart that succumbs to such bizarre activity. Let us learn forever that the simple truth of the gospel is enough to do it all.

I Saw Him Do It

The claim to special discoveries promises to become more widespread and even more exotic than it is now. Indeed, this development is happening before our eyes. We live in the day of the conquest of space and great attention to the heavens. Therefore, the demented mind has additional phenomena about which to invent unusual things. The addition of a "cosmic dimension" to cultic activity can safely be predicted. Indeed, the things of earth are getting somewhat prosaic with the cultic promoters, but now they have the latest rocket blast and the heavenly dimension to consider.

The pursuers of the "Heaven's Gate" cultic religion in southern California have become illustrations of this. The messianic leader promised that a spaceship was waiting for his followers just beyond a comet, newly arrived from outer space. His prediction was convincing enough that 38 members gathered together to drink poison and, as a result, passed from this world. Can we imagine anyone so gullible as to believe a promise such as this? The answer is yes—providing the individual has already been corrupted and subverted by false doctrine. That which is false, when pursued, leads deeper into bizarre thinking and dangerous actions. To believe doctrine that is false is very serious and, as our generation proves, it can be fatal. The problem continues, however, and all that one must do is to discover another spaceship that no one else can see, and presto! the crowd turns in that direction. It certainly goes without saying that both the crowd and the religious community need a new injection of "sanctified cynicism" in order to face an increasingly beguiling set of discoveries in the future.

I also suggest that the developments in the field of television will become a significant promotional item for special discoveries. The marriage of the computer and the television screen makes it possible for almost anything to be presented to people as fact or as truth. Take, for example, the calling down of fire from heaven. Many commercials and the films they promote are characterized by a bursting flame, tremendous explosions, and fire everywhere. It looks as if individuals are being consumed by the flame, but then they walk out safely (sometimes to our amazement). The flaming destruction was simply a computer-generated combination of images made to appear on the television screen. The thing we were so sure we were seeing in reality never really existed.

It is noted in Scripture that the "false prophet" will indeed be able to call down fire from heaven in the sight of people. In addition, he can work related false miracles to heighten the impression. We can "prove" the possibility of this by looking at our modern computer-generated graphics. The image on the screen seems so real that the easily led may become totally convinced in a moment of time. It is almost as if technology is creating phenomenalistic tools the Antichrist can use to try to deceive the elect. "I saw him do it!" may be the testimony of the self-deceived. "He was on my own television set!" is the cry of

the duped. So it is that "special discoveries" can be manu-
factured in great numbers out of thin air, and the ultimate
product will be verified by those willing to testify that "it
seemed so real."

Virtual Reality

A new creation in this regard also comes in the form of
holograms. One need only visit one of the theaters in
Branson, Missouri, or several other places to see this phenomena. Smoke is produced in the air, then laser lights
from the four corners of the auditorium produce in that
smoke what appears to be a living image. Words become
suspended in mid-air, and human or animal images appear.
The effect is startling. Virtual reality may seem like an inno-
cent game on the part of some, but it can be used to create
dreadful images to take the place of the real person or
events.

This development is heightened by the fact that many
are instantly willing to believe virtual reality in contrast to
genuine reality. But, alas, we cannot forget the warning of
Christ that spiritual subversion will become convincing at
the end of the age: "For false Christs and false prophets will
arise and will show great signs and wonders, so as to mislead, if possible, even the elect" (Matthew 24:24). Let us
never forget that the Bible predicts increased forms of spiritual subversion and multiplied ways to deceive the unwary.
Remember the key question "By what authority do you
speak?" should be asked of every person claiming special
insight. It is possible to predict with little fear of contradic-
tion that attractive, new special discoveries will appear as if
by magic on the religious scene. When we remember that
the Scripture predicts that ultimately "the whole earth will
worship Satan" (Revelation 13:10), we do well to look for
the development of virtual reality used to promote religious

phenomena in our time. When we see such a warning that a satanic religion is going to take over the world before the end comes, we should be exceedingly careful. We must remind ourselves again that cultic promotion is not just silly talk or fun and games. It is a deadly serious event.

The Deceivers

Concerning false teachers, the Bible warns of many people being led astray. Like a spiritual cancer, cultic thinking will move in to supplant sound doctrine in the minds of the unwary. There will be satanic religion in the last days. What will characterize this terrible time? The Bible warns of at least seven traits. The announcement of these seven elements is preceded by the statement that Satan will know his time is short and go forth with great wrath to work his dreadful things in the minds of people (see Revelation 12:12). The presentation of that last-days satanic religion is a gripping one in the Word of God. Revelation 13 gives us a clear delineation of the way it will be. That evil religion will be:

1. *Satanic:* Revelation 13:4 tells us the people of earth "worship the dragon." We have had enough experience with cults in our time to know the dreadful implication of a full-blown religion centered around Satan. Many a naïve pursuant of Satan has ended up in a graveyard.

2. *Humanistic:* That same verse also tells us that the people of earth will "worship the beast." The beast is a human being—the Antichrist who sets himself up as a false messiah. Worship of the Antichrist adds a dreadful humanism to that satanic religion.

3. *Universal:* It will be a religion practiced by the whole earth (Revelation 13:3). The satanic religion will embrace everyone to the very ends of the earth.

4. *Ecumenical:* We are told that every person on earth "shall worship him." We can, therefore, expect a religion to appear that will present the lowest common denominator for people to believe. One can only imagine what the unifying feature of such a religion will be. A look at history shows us that many religions had strange unifying features—all the way from total asceticism to sexual orgies.

5. *Phenomenalistic:* Describing that religion, the Scriptures offer details about its leader, an individual called the false prophet:

> And he exercises all the authority of the first beast in his presence. And he makes the earth and those who dwell in it to worship the first beast, whose fatal wound was healed. And he performs great signs, so that he even makes fire come down out of heaven to the earth in the presence of men. And he deceives those who dwell on the earth because of the signs which it was given him to perform in the presence of the beast, telling those who dwell on the earth to make an image to the beast who had the wound of the sword and has come to life (Revelation 13:12-14).

Amazing miracles will come and will appear to validate the power of the false prophet. Our world waits to be impressed by such striking phenomena.

6. *Idolatrous:* An image will be created about which the Scripture says, "And there was given to him to give breath to the image of the beast, that the image of the beast might even speak and cause as many as do not worship the image of the beast to be killed" (Revelation 13:15). So we have an idolatrous relationship in which the world is called to fall before the image of the Antichrist. Even so, in many a theme park today we have contraptions that look almost like human beings, be they robots or holograms. We are coming close to the place where the appearance of life can come from a mechanical device.

7. Cruelty: Those who choose not to worship the image of the beast will be condemned to death. It is difficult to imagine a religion so cruel that the penalty for not believing in its preposterous precepts is physical death. But this is the gross and insensate final result of false doctrine. Lest we say that such a thing is impossible, let's remember that many "religions" in our present world have had the same penalty. For instance, Aleksandr Solzhenitsyn tells us that 60 million were killed by communist leaders—millions of their own people slaughtered for not accepting the communist party line. Mussolini did the same thing to his people, as did Hirohito. Saddam Hussein has done the same. The combination of a presumptuous messianic leader, false doctrine, and a gullible constituency produces terrible results. These grim events will embrace the whole world in the last days.

Very close to the claim of special discoveries is a form of idolatry that is practiced by the cults already: the worship of "things." Because people desire to revere something they can see, they are prone to accept the vesting of respect, divine presence, or unusual capability that is ascribed to some physical object. Christians must remind themselves constantly that the Scripture says, ".While we look not at the things which are seen, but at the things which are not seen; for the things which are seen are temporal, but the things which are not seen are eternal" (2 Corinthians 4:18). The things which are *not* seen are the reality of Christianity, rather than the things which *are* seen.

Therefore we should flee like the plague an announcement of any kind of divine presence or divine blessing in a physical object. This goes for all statues, all "pieces of the cross," all uniforms, all rings, pens, pins, pocket coins, jeweled crosses, and the like. Millions of pieces of religious paraphernalia have been concocted across the world to enhance the impact made by a given cult. Indeed, we surely move from Christian to cultic when we begin to place two pieces of metal on the wall and bow before it because we think of it being in the shape of the cross. The revering of physical things is idolatry, pure and simple.

The reality of Christianity is not kissing the toe of a statue. It is "Christ in you, the hope of glory" (Colossians 1:27). The reality of Christianity is *Jesus Christ Himself*—not a form that represents Him. Because Christ lives in our lives, He is not to be represented by an object.

The other evening I saw a television presentation that encouraged all the listeners to "buy a cross for $69.95." In the course of the 30-minute presentation, preposterous claims were made for what that cross "would do for you." Some movie stars, celebrities, and scores of interesting people were put on the screen in order to make the claim of this "unusual cross" and say how it will bring healing, hope, and peace of mind. The list of benefits was quite long. One can imagine how many gullible people sent money to these people in order to gain the "blessing" that cross would bring. But the blessing of the cross doesn't come for $69.95, nor does it arrive in a box through the mail. *It comes by grace,* and includes the forgiveness of every sin and the fellowship of Jesus Christ as personal Savior. We move from reality to cheap logic when we foster other things as being the essence of spirituality. Beware of symbols. Without caution a Christian may move from the symbol to the substance.

STUDY QUESTIONS

1. What blessing does Bible study bring to the life of a believer?

2. What information has God already given us, according to 2 Peter 1:3,4?

3. How is the Christian faith free from secret knowledge and uncomfirmable relationships? How does that differ from many cults?

4. What warning does Christ give in Matthew 24:23-26?

5. If someone told you they had a computer code that could discern the "secret, encoded messages of Scripture," how would you respond to them?

The Wrong View of Jesus

Who is Jesus Christ?

This is the most important question any person will ever face. The deepest joys we will ever know in this life *and* our very hope of eternal life depend on the proper answer. Because this is true, we may be sure that the primary activity of Satan will be to obscure as much as possible the true nature of the person of our blessed Savior, the Lord Jesus.

In the entire history of the church, the most grievous heresies have been those that have advocated a view of Christ other than that which is taught in the Word of God. Satan knows that an improper understanding of the person and work of Christ makes salvation impossible.

The attack on the understanding of the nature of Christ began in the days of the early church. The intellectually disposed Colossians began to be infected by a heretical view called *Gnosticism*. This doctrinal error taught that a human approached the Godhead through progressive steps of higher and higher angelic beings who bridged the gap between man and God. Gnostics taught that Christ was one of these angelic beings who was more than man but less than God. They advocated the worship of angelic beings and included worshiping Christ as merely part of the duty of a Christian.

The apostle Paul, knowing the peril the Colossians were facing by turning to a religion other than the faith of Jesus Christ, wrote them a most earnest epistle. He warned, "See to it that no one takes you captive through philosophy and empty deception, according to the tradition of men, according to the elementary principles of the world, rather than according to Christ. For in Him all the fulness of Deity dwells in bodily form" (Colossians 2:8,9). Paul expanded that warning into the details of their false religion by saying, "Let no one keep defrauding you of your prize by delighting in self-abasement and the worship of the angels, taking his stand on visions he has seen, inflated without cause by his fleshly mind, and not holding fast to the head, from whom the entire body, being supplied and held together by the joints and ligaments, grows with a growth which is from God" (Colossians 2:18,19).

These people prided themselves in possessing knowledge. Paul told them that knowledge was not enough; they must have "full knowledge." He insisted that this full knowledge was the knowledge of the person of Jesus Christ. The Scripture insists that in worshiping Jesus Christ, we are worshiping God: "He who does not honor the Son does not honor the Father who sent Him" (John 5:23).

Later in the history of the church there grew up another sub-Christian point of view called Arianism. This was one of the first heresies of the church, and it was declared so because it denied the true deity of the Lord Jesus Christ. The advocacy of Arianism by the satanic opponents of Christianity produced great doctrinal clarity in the ranks of the early Christians. These confrontations led them to the greatly reinforced conviction that one's attitude toward the nature of Jesus Christ is primary to Christianity. A false view of the Savior produced a false religion, which presented no salvation at all. This conviction led the early church fathers to earnestly contend for the faith. They knew what was at stake. The issue was the survival of Christianity.

What Do We Believe About Jesus?

So much historical precedent of cultic attacks on the person of Christ should make us not surprised at the cultic detractions today. Most of the cults that are active in our time deny the true deity of Christ, the true humanity of Jesus, or the true union of the two natures in one Person. Notice the confusing Christian Science view of our Lord Jesus:

> Jesus is the human man who demonstrated Christ. Christ is the ideal Truth, divine idea, the spiritual or true idea of God.

> Mary's conception of him was spiritual.

> Jesus was the offspring of Mary's self-conscious communion with God.

> At the ascension the human, material concept, or Jesus, disappeared, while the spiritual self, or Christ, continues to exist in the eternal order of divine Science, taking away the sins of the world, as the Christ has always done, even before the human Jesus was incarnate to mortal eyes.

> His resurrection was not bodily! He reappeared to his students, that is, to their apprehension he rose from the grave—on the third day of his ascending thought![5]

The Jehovah's Witnesses are just as confused. Here's what they say:

> Jesus Christ, a created individual, is the second greatest Personage of the universe, the first and only direct creation by his Father, Jehovah ...

appointed as His vindicator and the Chief Agent of life toward mankind.

As a human son of God, October, 2 B.C. Became the Messiah Seed in Fall, A.D. 29. Died on Stake as Ransomer in Spring A.D. 33. Resurrected Immortal on Third Day . . . He was raised "as a mighty immortal spirit Son" . . . a glorious spirit creature.

We know nothing about what became of (his body), except that it did not decay or corrupt.[6]

The Mormon church says:

Jesus Christ is Jehovah, the first-born among the spirit children of Elohim, to whom all others are juniors.

He is unique in that he is the offspring of a mortal mother and of an immortal, or resurrected and glorified, Father.

He was the executive of the Father, Elohim, in the work of creation.

He is greater than the Holy Spirit, which is subject unto him, but His Father is greater than He.[7]

The cultic views of modern liberal theology are little better. They speak of Jesus Christ as an idyllic figure, the flower of humanity, and the world's greatest ethical teacher. A man so good his deluded followers took him for a god. Jesus, according to the cultists was divine—and therefore, in the same sense, all are divine. The spark of divinity only needs to be fanned into flame. In Christ, according to this thinking, humanity was divinity and divinity was humanity.

In attempting to explain Him, sub-Christian thinking has to create excuses for His life and work. Thus we find descriptions that proclaim, "The recorded miracles of Christ are merely legendary exaggerations of events that are entirely explicable from natural causes," and "Jesus spoke in accommodation with the ideas of His contemporaries and held the current Jewish notions." One cultist wrote that "Christ was a master product of evolution." And rejecting God's revealed history of Christ's miraculous birth, one self-proclaimed expert noted that, "those who recorded the virgin birth were doubtless influenced by pagan fables, thinking thus to secure for Him the honor of celestial paternity. A virgin birth and literal resurrection are no essential part of Christian faith."

The fevered minds of the Theosophy people have produced the following: "Jesus gave to the world fragments of teaching of value as basis for world religion, as did men like Buddha, Confucius, Pythagoras, and others . . . At a certain stage in the career of Jesus, the latter was taken possession of by the great Teacher, the Bodhisattva of eastern tradition."[8]

The central truth of Christianity is therefore related to the question, "What think ye of Christ?" The Christian is commanded to test the spirits of these suspicious alternative messengers. The doctrinal test of those spirits is very clear: "Beloved, do not believe every spirit, but test the spirits to see whether they are from God; because many false prophets have gone out into the world. By this you know the Spirit of God: every spirit that confesses that Jesus Christ has come in the flesh is from God; and every spirit that does not confess Jesus is not from God; and this is the spirit of the antichrist, of which you have heard that it is coming, and now it is already in the world" (1 John 4:1-3).

It is clear then that the test of a true representative of the gospel has to do with his definition of the person and the work of Jesus Christ. The central doctrine of Christianity is *Christology*, the doctrine of the nature of the person of Jesus Christ.

The God-Man

Christianity affirms both the true *deity* and the true *humanity* of our blessed Savior, whose divine and human nature is conjoined together in one personality (hypostatic union). By this we understand that Jesus Christ was not partly man and partly God on the basis of some percentage or formula. He is *true* humanity. He is *true* deity in human form—the God-man. One characteristic of biblical faith is that it has a proper understanding of the nature of the person of Christ.

Many today who claim to be Christians deny the true deity of Christ. Religious liberalism can be judged as heretical on the basis of its denial of the sure deity of the blessed Son of God. Liberalism is not Christianity, it is a heretical, anti-Christian view, being defective in its view of the Lord's deity.

Certain so-called Christian religions also deny the true humanity of the Savior. Christian Science, for instance, denies the existence of the physical, claiming that the essential substance of the universe is mind. "All is mind" is the index of Mary Baker Eddyism. If the physical does not exist, then deity did not become true humanity in the person of Christ. This is the doctrine of Antichrist, according to Scripture.

The thoughtful Christian will carefully analyze the doctrine of the cult that is being pressed upon him, paying special attention to the Christology of that alternative religious teaching. The message that declares Christ to be the automaton of the Father and not a real person in Himself is a cult. The message that denies the virgin birth of Christ, holding Him to be merely the natural son of Joseph and Mary, is a cult. An examination of the doctrinal base of any religion in the light of its views on the person and the work of Jesus Christ can be most revealing.

The question "What think ye of Jesus?" is only answered correctly by the believing Christian. In agreement with an ancient creed, the Christian gladly answers,

> Jesus Christ is the only begotten Son of the living God, God incarnate in the form of human flesh. He is the Son of man, the only Savior of the world, the Author and Finisher of our faith, who, through His death on the cross, provides redemption for all who believe in Him. He is the One who died for our sins, rose again on the third day, who lives to make intercession for us before His Father and who one day will come in His glorious returning to judge the quick and the dead at His appearing in His kingdom. He is Lord and God, and in Him alone we have life, and life more abundantly.

The Tri-Unity of God

Closely related to the fatal heresy of defective Christology is a denial of the *trinity* of the Godhead. The only true God is one God, eternally existent in three persons: Father, Son, and Holy Spirit. Each person of the Godhead is coequal and coeternal with the others. This view is not held by the Jehovah's Witnesses, who say:

> The Word of God gives no authority for the doctrine of the Trinity of the Godhead.

> The Trinity doctrine is unbiblical in origin.

> Rebellion in Eden called into question Jehovah's position as supreme sovereign. The Scriptures abound with evidence that the primary issue before creation is the vindication of name and Word.

> God is a solitary being form, unrevealed and unknown. No one has existed as His equal to reveal Him.

> Jehovah is the almighty and supreme Sovereign of the universe—not omnipresent, but with power extending everywhere.[9]

Many cults are blind to the nature of God, and in their theology they deny the deity of Jesus Christ or the deity of the Holy Spirit. An improper faith in the only true God makes impossible any real hope of salvation. These critical doctrinal problems concerning the nature of the Godhead should come to each Christian as a new reminder of the need for Christian scholarship. For too long we have been influenced by foolish leaders who say, "We don't need doctrine; we just need experience!" In the same vein is the mindless claim, "We don't preach doctrine, we just preach Christ!" Preachers who talk like this need to move up from their spiritual kindergartens and realize the shameful neglect of their own personal scholarship and the consequent neglect of doctrinal preaching to their people. The cults will have a field day in exploiting experience-oriented saints who have no time for the study of Christian doctrine.

Who Do You Say That I Am?

We cannot overemphasize the importance of a proper understanding of the person of Jesus Christ. There are awesome beneficent consequences to believing correctly in the Lord Jesus. Conversely, there are eternally tragic results from ignorance of His person or any form of rejection of Him. In the Scripture, we have an account that points up this vastly important fact:

> Now when Jesus came into the district of Caesarea Philippi, He began asking His disciples, saying, "Who do people say that the Son of Man is?" And they said, "Some say John the Baptist; and others, Elijah; but still others, Jeremiah, or one of the

prophets." He said to them, "But who do you say
that I am?" And Simon Peter answered and said,
"Thou art the Christ, the Son of the living God."
And Jesus answered and said to him, "Blessed are
you, Simon Barjona, because flesh and blood did
not reveal this to you, but My Father who is in
heaven. And I also say to you that you are Peter,
and upon this rock I will build My church; and the
gates of Hades shall not overpower it" (Matthew
16:13-18).

The meaning of this important exchange has awesome
consequences for us all. Note that Peter had the proper
answer to the question, "But who do you say that I am?"
Peter immediately acknowledged Jesus as the Christ, the
Son of God. It is this statement to which Jesus was referring
when he said, "Upon this rock will I build my church." The
rock on which Christ promised to build His church and
effect the world of every age until His return was the rock
of that testimony—the fact that Jesus is the Messiah, the
Son of God. Down through the quickly passing ages of
church history, we have seen Christ fulfill this promise in His
church at all times.

A brief look around will confirm the validity of this
promise. What kind of church prospers? What sort of spiritual institution flourishes under the blessing of God? The
answer is before us in Scripture: the enterprise that holds
to the core truth that Jesus Christ is the Son of God and
Savior of the world. The converse is also true. The entity,
usually cultic, that denies the deity of Jesus Christ is certain
to wither and die. The deity of Jesus Christ is, therefore, the
most important doctrine of the church.

A warning can be lifted at this point. In cities, towns,
and villages are empty buildings called churches that once
were something special. They were important to the life of

the community and produced salvation and vital Christian living in every place where they were established. Now these buildings are hollow shells, mute testimony of a blessing that once was and now is gone. *Ichabod, the glory has departed,* has been written over the doorway and nobody comes anymore. The public press even comments on what it calls the mainline denominations and shows how they are a pale shadow of their former selves. Why is the glory departed? What happened to kill the life of these churches? The answer is very simple: *religious liberalism.* The essential doctrine of religious liberalism denies, rejects, or simply minimizes the person of Jesus Christ and the vital doctrine of His deity. Christ has promised to build His church on the testimony of the deity of Christ. Conversely, it is obvious that where His deity is denied there is no longer a vital testimony for the Lord. Every church in the world would do well to take a long, hard look at what has happened to liberal Christianity. Decline and demise are the words that point to them.

A lesson can be learned as well concerning the church that Christ purchased with His own blood. So long as it stands for the Book, the blood, and the blessed hope, it will know the blessing of God, and it will flourish. The secret of a successful church is not some obscure principle that requires research. It is the preaching and teaching of the Word of God and the constant reminder that He is the One who stands behind it all. To forget this is spiritual death. To remember this is to produce a flourishing testimony for the Lord Jesus in the midst of a cynical world.

We must ask of every person with a suspicious doctrine, "Who is Jesus Christ?" Then we must listen carefully. If the answer implies that Christ is less than God, let the speaker be anathema.

STUDY QUESTIONS

1. What are ten things you know for certain about Jesus Christ?

2. If someone told you that Jesus was not God, what would you say?

3. How would you respond if someone argued that Jesus was not really a man?

4. On what is the church built, according to Matthew 16:13-18?

5. What evidence do we have that a poor Christology leads to the ruination of the church?

Cut Off from the Truth

There is no book in all the world like the Bible.

The Word of God is the most interesting and inspiring reading available. It contains many high points of eloquence, illumination, and insight. It tells of the ministry of prophets, apostles, and other inspired men and women who were servants of God. Varying points of emphasis in the Bible strike responsive notes in the different personalities of the readers. The inevitable result is that each of us has favorite passages of Scripture—portions of the Word of God that were used to meet particular needs at given times. There is nothing wrong with this.

People of a loving disposition are thrilled with 1 Corinthians 13. Those who are judgmental in character enjoy reading 2 Thessalonians 1 or certain passages in Revelation. Christians with a historical bent are drawn to the passages of the Old Testament which describe the kings and kingdoms of antiquity. Those of philosophic interest enjoy the didactic conversations of Christ in the gospels and the logical discourses of Paul. Activists consider the great commission the most relevant passage of Scripture, often feeling that theological discussion on the nature of faith is a colossal waste of time. One can begin to get off base this way.

There are also people who are interested only in semantics. To them, the study of the Word of God is a perpetual game of anagrams. They are constantly counting verses and letters and attributing to them numerical value. They study the Word of God with a dictionary in one hand and a slide rule in the other. Semanticists are often frightened by the spiritual gladiators who read the book of Acts as a story of heroic conquest and feel constrained to go and do likewise.

The Bible is also read by sociologist types. These people may forever discuss the religio-economic trends that were established by the density of the population of the city of Jerusalem as influenced by the Christian subculture and populatively aerated by the early persecutions. They are worried about those who concentrate on Paul's description of this life as being a "momentary, light affliction . . . producing for us an eternal weight of glory far beyond all comparison" (2 Corinthians 4:17). The sociological Christians accuse such ones as being "so heavenly minded they are no earthly good." They warn that Christianity is more than pie-in-the-sky and consists essentially in loving one's brother and revealing such love.

Those disposed to see in the Bible a delineation of forms of worship range from the most informal Quakers to high-church Episcopalians. One's emotional disposition affects his convictions as to the teaching of Scripture. Episcopalians from their high-church position cannot tell the difference between the Baptists and the Brethren, and the Pietists believe Episcopalians are Catholics who flunked Latin. Human dispositions, responding to the portions of Scripture to which they have given attention, have made of this amorphous thing called "Christianity" a crazy quilt of groups whose resemblance is obscure indeed. There are enough differences between believers that if they were properly exploited the church could become a hotbed of Christian charity! The admonition to keep the unity of the Spirit in the bond of peace is important in light of the variety of groups, experiences, and emphases that come under the heading "Christian."

Variation in the Church

Many organizationally disposed individuals can hardly forgive the Holy Spirit for manifesting Himself in diversity and not in uniformity. But the diversity of Christian groups is sometimes a good thing and not without the permission of our heavenly Father. Variation and diversity are not marks of error.

But herein lies a potentially serious problem. The temptation of groups of serious conviction is to move ever further from the central pale of reason that C.S. Lewis calls "mere Christianity." Because of their emphasis, they begin declaring that "love is everything" or "history is all-important." They take some important but not critical emphasis of Scripture and move it to the exalted position of imperative doctrine. They move their test of fellowship away from the person of Jesus Christ to some lesser point. Soon wearing a given kind of clothing, visiting the mother church, or some other distinctive becomes a test of fellowship. Such a group may have started well, but for want of proper attention to the whole counsel of God they drift away from vital Christianity.

It is easy to see how a religious group can move from the true to the false by small steps of defection from the teaching of Holy Scripture. The special emphases of many religious groups have been helpful to Christianity. Too often, however, the special emphasis becomes the critical, all-important point. When a theological eccentricity moves to the very center of the attention of a group of Christians, that group, often without sensing it, becomes potentially heretical. Once we move away from the clear teaching of

Scripture, we run the risk of becoming cut off from the truth.

This "outward bound" direction must always be avoided by the biblical Christian. When a group develops a theological or doctrinal interpretation that touches only minimally on the proper biblical emphasis and lives for the most part outside of that circle, it becomes a cult. By this I mean that, from a starting point of Scripture, it has moved away from the teaching of the Word of God so that its central emphasis has become a set of human philosophies, ideas, or revelations that can no longer be justified biblically. A cult's attention to an interesting portion of Scripture has been carried to the point where it has isolated that passage of the Word of God from the corrective modifications found in other portions of the Word.

Segmented Biblical Attention

Virtually every cult in existence today has followed the unwise course of segmented biblical attention beyond the pale of reason into the production of a destructive heresy. We have an illustration of this in the Word of God. It involves an encounter between the apostle Paul and a group that knew only the baptism of John:

> And it came about that while Apollos was at Corinth, Paul having passed through the upper country came to Ephesus, and found some disciples, and he said to them, "Did you receive the Holy Spirit when you believed?"
>
> And they said to him, "No, we have not even heard whether there is a Holy Spirit."
>
> And he said, "Into what then were you baptized?"
>
> And they said, "Into John's baptism."

And Paul said, "John baptized with the baptism of repentance, telling the people to believe in Him who was coming after him, that is, in Jesus." And when they heard this, they were baptized in the name of the Lord Jesus. And when Paul had laid his hands upon them, the Holy Spirit came on them, and they began speaking with tongues and prophesying (Acts 19:1-6).

Here is the account of disciples who heard and gladly responded to the inspired preaching of John the Baptist. They embraced with sincerity his doctrine of repentance for the remission of sins, "for the kingdom of heaven is at hand" (Matthew 3:2). They became disciples of John the Baptist, and we may well assume that they continued faithfully in their conviction of the truth of the message of this humble forerunner of Jesus Christ.

But herein was their problem. They were so taken with the preaching of John that they neglected his major emphasis: "It is He who comes after me, the thong of whose sandal I am not worthy to untie" (John 1:27). They missed the opportunity to hear the Word of Christ! They missed the chance to believe in Him and become true Christians, sharing in the gift of the Holy Spirit given to the church on the day of Pentecost. Their own testimony was that they had not even heard of the Holy Spirit.

These people had not come to the place where they shared the life of God that comes to every person who is made a new creature in Jesus Christ. The apostle Paul's question to these disciples, "Did you receive the Holy Spirit when you believed?" was a most appropriate way of asking whether they had become true Christians. Realizing that they were not indeed believers, the apostle Paul said to them that they should believe on "Him who should come after" John the Baptist. They should receive Jesus Christ.

The happy conclusion of this story is that they did indeed believe on Jesus, were baptized in His name, and received the gift of the Holy Spirit.

We may rejoice that Paul was given the opportunity to bring to these sincere seekers after truth the final revelation of God in Jesus Christ. It is highly probable that they would otherwise have followed a religious group centered around the preaching of John the Baptist, which, however sincere, would have prevented people from hearing the true message of salvation. Their sincere attention to a segmented, nonfinal revelation would have kept them from eternal life through Christ. Their religious beliefs and practices would have been merely cultic rather than real and vital Christianity.

Listening to the Entire Word

The lesson for all of us is very clear. While we may be fascinated with the words of one of the personalities of Scripture and with the emphasis of a given book of the Bible, we must not fail to pay attention to the message of the *entire* Word of God. The Bible declares that *all* Scripture is given by inspiration of God and is profitable for training and correcting the people of God (2 Timothy 3:16,17). It is of great importance that the doctrine by which a Christian orients his faith and his life come from *all* Scripture. He must remember that the Bible, both Old and New Testaments, was given by inspiration of the Holy Spirit and is vital in its entirety to a Christian understanding of the faith. He remembers also that revelation is progressive. God presented truth in a cumulative fashion, moving from the basic theistic concepts of the Old Testament to the final revelation of Himself in Jesus Christ. Christ brought life and immortality to light through the gospel, and His doctrine was explained to us by His apostles who wrote the letters of the New Testament.

We must never forget that the proper interpretation of the Bible must be based on text, context, and greater context. The biblical interpreter must ask, "What does this verse mean? In what setting is it given to us? How does it relate to the whole Bible?"

The major deficiency of the cults of our time is that they have neglected to base their faith on the Bible as a whole. One group denies the immortality of the soul because of a statement about death in Ecclesiastes 9:5. They ignore the fact that the final light on the subject of immortality was given to us by Jesus Christ. Paul explains that to be absent from the body is to be present with the Lord (see 2 Corinthians 5:8). The Way, a cultic fringe of the Jesus movement, denies the existence of the trinity because of an undue emphasis on the personality of Jesus. The result of this doctrinal disorientation is that this group seems to settle for a psychological encounter with the personality of Jesus as the basis of salvation.

The transcendental meditation people make the same mistake. They read verses in the Bible on thinking and meditating, and the rest they get from an Indian guru. Putting their minds into neutral, they suppose that they can think and meditate on nothing and get definitive answers. Some very strange personalities have resulted from religions so transcendental that they never touch the ground of a real world. Meditation in moderation is fine, but there comes a time when we must also go to work. One editorial writer helpfully analyzed the "Children of God" cult as follows:

> The Children's tendency to bend the Bible to fit
> their own whims smacks of cultism and leads to
> dangerously blind spots in crucial realms of life.
> They presumptuously accuse Paul of having been

out of God's will whenever he worked at tent-making. (No one has yet suggested this of Christ, who during His "silent years" presumably worked as a carpenter for pay.) The Children need to be more honest in their use of Scripture. A greater understanding and appreciation of hermeneutics would help.[10]

Some who pretend to be experts on demonism fall into the same error. Knowing of demon influence, they proceed to attribute all forms of aberrant behavior to the presence of Satan's minions. The final consequence is that laziness, lust, clock-watching, loud talking, and all other irresponsible activities are thought to be the result of demonic influence.

There are others who find a verse in the Bible about God having given to some prophet a vision. They use this as the scriptural base for a notion that all sound religion is therefore conducted on the basis of God revealing Himself in visions and dreams. Such a notion can cause a person to drift away from the Word of God and into a spiritual opium den of his own making.

Another leader may greatly encourage Christians by his emphasis on a relaxed and positive mental attitude. While this message may be of value, if taken as ultimate truth, it can cause a naïve person to finally deny physical reality. No mental attitude can take away the fact of death or deliver us from the necessity of living in the midst of physical dimensions. A positive mental attitude is good when properly applied. At other times it is mere foolishness.

The mature Christian will make none of these mistakes. He will continue in a daily study of the Word of God and apply the teachings of Scriptures in the place and to the degree in which God intended them to be applied. He knows the danger of twisting the Scripture. He will avoid the

dreaded pitfalls of spiritual lunacy that come from depart-
ing the faith on the basis of any one verse in the Bible.

The Promises of Scripture

It is a grave temptation for any group to find a verse in
the Bible about holiness, the kingdom, law, grace, works,
faith, or something else and use it for a substitute for the
whole counsel of God. Even zealous Christians have frequently fallen into the trap of segmented biblical interpretation, thereby creating a cultic influence in their system of
doctrine. Christian maturity will save us from all of this.

These things having been said, a word of caution may
be appropriate. It is true that some parts of the Word of
God, some chapters and verses of Holy Scripture, apply
more directly to certain situations and specific people than
others. We must be careful about inventing a "flat-book
hermeneutic," lending the same importance to one passage as we do to another. One frequently sung chorus said,
"Every promise in the book is mine, every chapter, every
verse, every line. All are blessings of His love divine; every
promise in the book is mine." While this chorus was popular, it is not, in fact, exactly true. God, for instance, spoke
to Abraham in a certain place in the Old Testament and
said to him, "Go forth from your country, and from your
relatives and from your father's house, to the land which I
will show you; and I will make you a great nation, and I will
bless you, and make your name great; and so you shall be
a blessing; and I will bless those who bless you, and the
one who curses you I will curse. And in you all the families
of the earth shall be blessed" (Genesis 12:1-3). We read
these verses with appreciation and thank God for the
promise He made to Abraham. We instantly recognize,
however, that the promise was made to *Abraham* and not to
us. This promise was a foundation stone of the people of

Israel, given to Abraham and his seed. We cannot claim these promises for ourselves. Similarly, God one day spoke to the nation of Israel saying, "And they shall live on the land that I gave to Jacob My servant, in which your fathers lived; and they will live on it, they, and their sons, and their sons' sons, forever; and David My servant shall be their prince forever" (Ezekiel 37:25). That was a promise given by God to a specific individual, at a specific time, in a specific situation. To claim it for ourselves is illogical.

Again and again, we find in the pages of the Old Testament promises given to various groups and individuals. It is necessary for the scholarly reader of the Bible to be discerning about the relevance of a given promise. In fact, concerning every statement in Scripture, we must ask questions such as: Who is making this promise? To whom is the promise made? Under what circumstances was the promise made? Asking these simple questions will save believers from a great deal of spiritual confusion. Keeping our eyes on the biblical Jesus and maintaining our faith in Him will protect us from the snares and subterfuges of the cults.

STUDY QUESTIONS

1. What is wrong with building an entire belief system on one short passage of Scripture? How can paying special attention to one portion of Scripture cut us off from the body of divine truth?

2. How is that demonstrated in Acts 19:1-6?

3. How could it be a good thing that the Holy Spirit has allowed a diversity of Christian groups?

4. What does 2 Timothy 3:16,17 teach us about the value of God's Word?

5. "The major deficiency of the cults is that they have neglected to base their faith on the Bible as a whole." Do you agree or disagree with that statement? Why? What evidences or examples can you offer to support your answer?

Slaves to the Structure

"You belong to me!"

While these are not exactly the words of a grand old hymn, this is a song title that nicely represents the point of view of almost every cult leader. Cults actually bring their followers into psychological and spiritual slavery.

A very interesting description of the believer in Jesus Christ is found in our Lord's statement, "The wind blows where it wishes and you hear the sound of it, but do not know where it comes from and where it is going; *so is everyone who is born of the Spirit*" (John 3:8, emphasis added). We may well sympathize with the response of Nicodemus, the well-organized Jewish religionist, when he asked, "How can these things be?" Nicodemus was astonished with the assertion of Jesus Christ about the necessity of the new birth and with this remarkable statement of Christian freedom.

This same theme—the freedom of the person who has become a believer in Jesus Christ—is echoed throughout the New Testament. In John 8:36 we read, "If therefore the Son shall make you free, you shall be free indeed." The apostle Paul strikes a similar theme when he writes, "Where the Spirit of the Lord is, there is liberty" (2 Corinthians 3:17). In another passage, he warns of losing our liberty to those who would enslave: "You were bought with a price; do not become slaves of men" (1 Corinthians 7:23). So important to the writers of Scripture is the preservation of Christian freedom that we are not only advised that we possess it, but we are carefully warned never to lose it. In Galatians 5:1 Paul says, "It was for freedom that Christ set us free; therefore, keep standing firm and do not be subject again to a yoke of slavery." In that same passage, Paul explained that we must work to avoid entanglement in the yoke of bondage, stating, "You were called to freedom, brethren" (verse 13).

The consequent emphasis of the New Testament is that Christian leaders who have power or persuasive ability must be careful never to overly control or dominate the faith of others. The apostle Paul never said that the strong should *control* the weak, but rather that the strong should *support* the weak. No doubt there are and always will be individuals whose physical, mental, or spiritual inferiority make them vulnerable to the dominance of others. The religious leader has a solemn obligation to refuse to take advantage of that vulnerability. He must not use his gifts or talents as the leverage to power. He must avoid like the plague the temptation that will surely come to him to organize followers around himself rather than around Christ.

Leading by Example

A further expression of heartfelt concern regarding the attitude of leadership comes from the apostle Peter to the elders of the churches. Few passages are more indicative of the divine concern for the proper pastoral attitude than his earnest words, "Shepherd the flock of God among you, exercising oversight not under compulsion, but voluntarily, according to the will of God; and not for sordid gain, but with eagerness; nor yet as lording it over those allotted to your charge, but proving to be examples to the flock" (1 Peter 5:3).

The Word of God is clear: Spiritual leadership is to be leadership by example. In simplicity and godly sincerity, the leader is to be an imitator of Jesus Christ and pray that his very life will furnish, before his onlooking flock, an illustration of the Christian life for all to see. When the life of a Christian leader illustrates only arrogance, groundless authoritarianism, and human imposition, he is representing a different Christ than the one presented in Holy Scripture.

The apostle John, in his third epistle, may well be presenting a vignette of a leader whose life was characterized by such dreadful presumption. After calling himself simply a "fellow helper to the truth," John says, "I wrote something to the church; but Diotrephes, who loves to be first among them, does not accept what we say" (verse 9). Here was a leader who was inclined more toward preeminence than piety. The result is that he became an illustration, mentioned by name in Holy Scripture, of the kind of leadership that Christians can do without.

The promoters of the cults don't obey the rules Scripture lays down for leaders. Indeed, they know that their success is directly dependent upon their ability to trap followers into a permanent entanglement. This association is almost invariably formed with the bonds of fear. The leader's preaching, teaching, and efforts are dedicated not to the production of individual competence and freedom on the part of his followers, but to create dependence. The leaders of the cults are working to promote slavery, not liberty. Thus an almost universal characteristic of the cults is the creation of a monolithic, merciless, and convoluted "church" structure. To cult leaders the purpose of a religious organization is not that it becomes a living segment of the body of Christ, but that it becomes a personally exploitable syndicate.

We have evidence of the beginning of such a tendency in the pages of the New Testament. In the book of Revelation

Christ brought specific messages to seven New Testament churches. An examination of these messages to the churches can give us a new reminder of the divine attitude toward local religious groups. Many of the compliments and criticisms of the seven churches of Asia Minor are most applicable to religious organizations in our day. Of particular note is the message given to the church at Ephesus. Here was a church commended by the Lord because of its many virtues. They were, however, at the starting point of spiritual defection. Despite this, they were given a compliment by the Lord Jesus: "Yet this you do have, that you hate the deeds of the Nicolaitans, which I also hate" (Revelation 2:6).

The time of the early church was an era that spawned a group described by the name *Nicolaitans*. This same group is mentioned in a further note to the churches, namely the one that was addressed to the church at Pergamos. That church had progressed farther along the path of spiritual deterioration, and so the mention of the Nicolaitans among this group came in a different form: "You also have some who in the same way hold the teaching of the Nicolaitans. Repent therefore; or else I am coming to you quickly, and I will make war against them with the sword of My mouth" (Revelation 2:15,16).

Who were the Nicolaitans? What were their deeds and their doctrine? We have only one definite indication as to the nature of this group, and that comes to us from the meaning of the word itself. The word *Nicolaitan* comes from two Greek words, *nicao,* which literally means "victory over" or "subjugation of," and *laos,* which means "the people." Apparently the Nicolaitans took great pains to try to force their leadership onto the first-century believers, working to bind them to their particular brand of works-based theology. The exaggerated distinction between "clergy" and "laity" had begun in the early stages of Christianity. Some were already thinking it spiritually necessary or practical to subjugate the people of God and become masters over them. (The "super-organizers" were already appearing in the days of early Christianity!) Already the laypeople were considered exploitable commodities to be mastered by their religious leaders.

We can well imagine the efficient organizers of the churches at Ephesus and Pergamos conversing: "Well, we obviously cannot trust the ignorant men and women who come to our church from the normal pursuits of life to study the Bible for themselves. It is surely *our* responsibility to interpret God for them. After all, that is the responsibility of our exalted leadership." You see, power corrupts. This is not only true in the realm of politics, but it is also tragically true in the area of religion.

We can be very sure of the attitude of God toward this program, since He complimented the church at Ephesus for literally *hating* the deeds of the Nicolaitans—the Lord even said, "I also hate" them. The Holy Spirit saw fit to restate this attitude when He talked about the development of the doctrine of the Nicolaitans, saying, "Which thing I hate." The religious ascendancy of a group of spiritual elitists over the masses is a program and a belief that is hated by God. We must not ignore the fact that this attitude on the part of God is twice mentioned in these messages to the churches. The Lord is emphasizing to us that the subjugation of people is despised by God.

The Structure Kills the Spirit

We may note also that the Nicolaitan trend was merely a set of deeds in the church at Ephesus. By the time we come to the church at Pergamos, however, what had been deeds had turned into doctrine. How quickly do people work to give official doctrinal sanction to activities which are merely personal or organizational inventions!

Religious institutions today are filled with whole sets of catechisms, disciplines, liturgies, and stated methods that are basically nothing but the doctrine of the Nicolaitans. Who can doubt that many of today's religious organizations are efforts to rally people around a central loyalty other than Jesus Christ? This was the criticism that was leveled against the otherwise commendable church at Ephesus. The Lord told them, "You have left your first love" (Revelation 2:4). The believers at Ephesus were warned that they had fallen away from God, and they must repent and return to Him or else their candlestick would be removed and its light of testimony extinguished. So it is that the landscape of western civilization today is dotted with dark, spectral church buildings—ancient artifacts that are nothing but the crumbled remains of a viable testimony that is no more. The program of subjugation of the people kills the true work of Christ.

This kind of murdering organizational structure is one of the reliable indexes of the cults of our time. The cult demands that its converts give total commitment to an entangling organization, enmeshing them in an impossible set of human expectations. Like a fly, they move into the web. Soon comes the spider.

Whatever else the cultic leaders may be, they are super-organizers. It is impossible for a cult to succeed without conserving its gains and enrolling its followers with increasingly demanding obligations to the leader and the organization. The cult is usually represented to the captured devotee as synonymous with the kingdom of God.

Devotion to the Irrational

One of the normal connotations of the word *cultic* is that of a passionate devotion to a cause—even to the point of the irrational. The cult hopes to bring its hapless followers to the place where they think of little else except their involvement with the movement and its human leader. The average cultist is as much a slave to his present religious involvement as he ever was to the sins of his former life. This was precisely the accusation that Christ leveled at the Pharisees: "Woe to you lawyers as well! For you weigh men down with burdens hard to bear, while you yourselves will not even touch the burdens with one of your fingers" (Luke 11:46). The leaders of cults are, in the words of the apostle Peter, "promising them freedom while they themselves are slaves of corruption; for by what a man is overcome, by this he is enslaved" (2 Peter 2:19).

The present-day group calling themselves the "Children of God" demand that their youthful followers rob their parents before disappearing into the folds of this cultic Jesus religion. Organizational initiation is followed by peer group pressure, until finally the pitiful devotee is terror-stricken at the prospect of dropping out of his suspicious entanglements. Similarly, the Worldwide Church of God repeatedly announced that all others beside the members of their group were lost for eternity. Certain large religious groups in the world, some of them thought of as legitimate, still preach the doctrine of damnation for all outside their particular organization.[11]

The Christian has been delivered from all such nonsense. He knows that the word *loyalty* is only applicable in a final sense when applied to our relationship to Jesus Christ. The devotion that Christians have for one another is in loving response to the indwelling Holy Spirit, not submission to an enslaving external organization.

It is a truism that the less truth a movement represents, the more highly it must organize. Truth has its own magnetism producing loyalty. The absence of truth makes necessary the application of the bonds of fear. A cultic leader may present his wares by saying, "Come to Jesus," but his real theme song is "You belong to me." The Christian is well advised to heed the advice of the apostle Paul: "It was for freedom that Christ set us free; therefore keep standing firm and do not be subject again to a yoke of slavery" (Galatians 5:1).

The only *imperative* membership that the true Christian recognizes is membership in the body of Christ. While he may belong to a group which places great emphasis on membership in the local church, being a Christian he places no confidence in this area as *the basis for his eternal life.* The perceptive Christian is a unique kind of individual in that he is unable to be "organized" in the same sense as others who place a life-and-death importance on their organizational involvement. Jesus Christ has set us free, and no one is entitled to take that freedom from us.

Entangling Organizations

Entangling organizational structure is an insidious development because it sometimes seems benign. Churches, organizations, and religious structures have developed many parallel programs to add extra reasons for individuals to be members and loyally serve. One is insurance programs. Who can deny that it is good for the leader of a group, the pastor, or the superintendent to have life and health insurance policies that are products of his organizational involvements? Were he to choose to leave, however, would he not lose all or part of this insurance protection? Therefore, even though he may contemplate stepping out of the bad theology and coercive programs of his organization, it soon becomes unthinkable. The organizers of various enterprises know this and therefore labor ambitiously to produce this extra tie of loyalty to the organization.

Retirement programs come in the same class. Later in life, the maturing Christian leader probably has thousands of dollars invested in his retirement program which he has anticipated using. Again, were he to decide against the theology of the organization, the finances can still be used to promote continued involvement. The liberal denominations of the United States have certainly kept this in mind with reference to thousands of pastors. Many would like to leave the group that has long since denied the faith, but financial considerations deter such a course of action. Without realizing the gradual development of the web, they have involved themselves in an entangling structure from which they cannot escape without great loss.

In addition to these programs, leaders are constantly thinking about other forms of organizational structures that can add to the solid composite nature of the group. Many formerly valid Christian enterprises remain tied together even though good theology has long since been sacrificed. So it is that programs that are *parallel* to the preaching of the gospel, but not a part of it, still produce their own form of spiritual entanglement. Were it not for parallel programs, it is certain that the liberal establishment would be far less powerful, if in existence at all.

The possibility of cultic entanglement is so real that the individual Christian should think twice about any form of membership, become a member of as few groups as possible, and be independent and creative. Pursuing another course could bring many forms of less-than-spiritual entrapment.

What About Traditions?

Entangling organizational structures can be enhanced by an amorphous concept called "heritage." There are Christian movements that are hundreds of years old. Their very antiquity—and the antiquated buildings in which they meet—can produce a pseudo-loyalty indeed. For purely emotional reasons, individuals have said, "I can't leave this liberal church because my grandparents attended here." One can hardly imagine a form of compromise more meaningless than this kind of loyalty. It can be safely said that few words are more overdone in the church of our day than is the word *heritage.* Many times, the word should be translated into "loyalty to something else besides the truth of Scripture."

Another form of entanglement comes under the form of *tradition.* One should be very suspicious of the use of the word because it usually means "anybody's guess as to what it used to be." We ought to view with a genuine questioning attitude anyone's assertion of what is really a "tradition." I know of more than one cultic denomination which routinely claims, "This is the way the early church did it" to buttress their heresy. Many times pseudo-scholars are presented as having done "careful research" on the way the Christian liturgy came together in the second century A.D. A great deal of boilerplate is produced in the name of tradition that has no connection with reality. Even if these assertions that "the early church did it this way" were true, we are still to be unimpressed with their validity today. The conduct of a worship service 2,000 years ago is not to bear a provable consequence in our lives today. The changeless and marvelous reality of the gospel is the sacred core of Christianity. That message which was "once delivered to the saints" is to be the theme of our preaching and the source of our power in all ages.

It is not as clear what we are supposed to do about the church. Therefore, individual churches have taken one form or another, styles of preaching have changed in a dozen different ways down through the years, and a hundred other innovations have come into our Christian conduct. We can be sure that in time even these will change, giving way to others. To insist on a mode of building or a manner of singing as being "just as important as the teaching of the Word" is very unbiblical. The message of the death, burial, and resurrection of Jesus Christ is the changeless reality. The forms of worship for the Christian cannot make that same claim.

Beware of tradition and heritage. They can readily take us from Christian to cultic. The Protestant Reformation began with the declaration of Martin Luther: "No man can command my conscience." That conviction still stands us in good stead.

STUDY QUESTIONS

1. What does John 8:36 and 2 Corinthians 3:17 reveal about the believer's freedom?

2. How does that freedom mesh with being a "bondservant of Jesus," as mentioned in Romans 1:1 and Galatians 1:10?

3. Why does God hate organizational structures like that of the Nicolaitans?

4. In what ways do cults enslave people?

5. How can church traditions or programs be bondage?

The Cost of the Cult

All this can be yours . . . when you pay the membership fee. . . .

The marvelous message of the gospel of Christ is that one may receive eternal salvation without money and without price. The New Testament Scriptures tell us that salvation comes to us as an absolutely free gift. The fact that it's a *gift,* rather than a purchase or wage, reveals the uniqueness of the Christian faith. "The *gift* of God is eternal life," we read in Romans 6:23 (emphasis added). We are "justified *freely* by His grace," it says in Romans 3:24 (emphasis added). The word *freely* literally means "without a cause." God has been gracious to us, not because we *earned* it, but because He is merciful and loving and it pleases Him to do so.

The grace of Jesus Christ is the all-pervading doctrine that applies both to the reception of salvation and our continued walk with God. By the grace of Jesus Christ, each of us as Christians has become rich: "For you know the grace of our Lord Jesus Christ, that though He was rich, yet for your sake He became poor, that you through His poverty might become rich" (2 Corinthians 8:9). The Christian is rich indeed! He has received the wonderful gift of justification by faith and a thousand attendant benefits. All of this comes to him because of the expenditure of the blood of Jesus Christ on Calvary's cross. The believer is who he is by the grace of God. All of those blessings are a free gift—none of it has been earned or paid for by the individual.

Buying God's Blessing?

The Word of God makes it clear that the Christian is never under obligation to do, give, sacrifice, or expend himself in any way in order to be more sure that he has the gift of God, which is eternal life. He is invited in many earnest ways to commit himself to the service of Christ and to become a useful instrument in the hands of God. The Bible is clear that service for Christ is a *voluntary proposition* on the part of the Christian, and nothing that he does will increase his guarantee of eternal life. He is saved by grace and kept by the power of God. His eternal life came to him without payment on his part. It is dependent on the work of Christ on the cross.

It is also clear in Scripture that the gifts, the power, and the blessing of God in the life of a Christian do not come because of one's ability to purchase them with money or because of his giving to God. We have a fascinating vignette in the book of Acts in which a man attempts to do exactly that. It seems that a man called Simon, who was previously involved in sorcery, became a believer in Jesus Christ. He saw the remarkable power of the apostles through the wonderful working of the Holy Spirit, and he immediately realized the possibilities in the use of such power:

> Now when Simon saw that the Spirit was bestowed through the laying on of the apostles' hands, he offered them money, saying, "Give this authority to me as well, so that everyone on whom I lay my hands may receive the Holy Spirit."

> But Peter said to him, "May your silver perish with you, because you thought you could obtain the gift

of God with money! You have no part or portion in this matter, for your heart is not right before God. Therefore repent of this wickedness of yours, and pray the Lord that if possible, the intention of your heart may be forgiven you. For I see that you are in the gall of bitterness and in the bondage of iniquity."

But Simon answered and said, "Pray to the Lord for me yourselves, so that nothing of what you have said may come upon me" (Acts 8:18-24).

Quite obviously the gifts and the power of God were not a purchasable commodity. Special blessing was hardly available to this man because of his financial offer. Indeed the opposite was true. Peter recognized the man's improper thinking and rebuked him in order to set him straight. And Simon responded appropriately, repenting of his sin and seeking to obey the Lord. One of the principles of that story is clear: We do not buy God's power and blessing. We have no teaching whatsoever in the New Testament that one develops an inside track with God or a greater certainty of salvation because of his giving.

The true leaders of the church were utterly offended at the suggestion that their favor or the favor of their God could be gained with money. They accused the one who made this offer of terrible sin and said he was surely under the judgment of God. We may thank the Lord that the apostles were really members of the "untouchables"—incorruptible people whose fidelity to Jesus Christ was beyond the power of money to buy. Indeed, in their ministries they spoke against the power of money again and again, saying finally, "The love of money is the root of all evil" (1 Timothy 6:10). They invited Christians to give gladly out of a pure heart, but they conducted their own lives on a plane of personal sacrifice. And they maintained utter rectitude as to the reception and the use of money.

They even went further than this. The early church fathers taught that sacrificial Christian leaders thereby gave evidence of their faithfulness to Jesus Christ. By contrast, they said that a characteristic of false teachers was that they "suppose that godliness is a means of gain" (1 Timothy 6:5). Peter, when speaking of false teachers, said, "In their greed they will exploit you with false words; their judgment from long ago is not idle, and their destruction is not asleep" (2 Peter 2:3).

The apostle Paul, again leaving us a shining example, was very careful never to accept gifts from the churches for his own personal use. He said, "You yourselves know that these hands ministered to my own needs and to the men who were with me. In everything I showed you that by working hard in this manner you must help the weak and remember the words of the Lord Jesus, that He Himself said, 'It is more blessed to give than to receive'" (Acts 20:34,35). Paul did this for the purpose of making the gospel of Jesus Christ totally without charge. The church of Christ is richer because of the peerless standard of personal sacrifice that was left for us by the apostles of Christ.

Happy is the Christian leader who at the end of his life can say with Paul, "I have coveted no one's silver or gold or clothes" (Acts 20:33). The apostle Paul both preached and practiced the proposition that the love of money is the root of all evil. What a contrast we see in the cultic practitioner of today! He strongly implies that money contributed to the cause will buy privileges or gifts or powers for the receptive follower. He offers healing for $100. He offers deliverance from accidents for life for $1,000. The follower of the cult is often promised that he can escape the many purgatories in this world and the next through the investment of his money.

Stealing from the Flock

In the financial structure of the average cult, tithing is but the beginning. Next comes the real pressure. The follower, as the screw is turned, is exploited to the point of economic exhaustion. The stories are legion of wives and children who have been brought to the point of hunger and impoverishment because of the cultic contributions of the head of the family. Enamored of his new spiritual leader, the head of the house forgets the clear teaching of Scripture, "If anyone does not provide for his own, and especially for those of his household, he has denied the faith, and is worse than an unbeliever" (1 Timothy 5:8).

Many cult leaders preach asceticism and penury, but refuse to live economically themselves. They steal from the flock, enriching their own pockets at the expense of their followers. The consequence is that conscienceless religious leaders have provided for themselves massive homes, spacious estates, and large holdings in the commercial world. Some of them even quote as their excuse, "No good thing will He withhold from them that walk uprightly" (Psalm 84:11). What is this but distorting the Scriptures to their own destruction?

The newspapers have carried many stories of shameless financial exploitation by cult leaders. Guru Maharaj Ji, arguing that he should be treated like a god, encourages lavish financial gifts to be given to him and his family. Herbert W. Armstrong pressed his followers to triple-tithe for the support of his cult. How else could private jets be purchased and operated for his personal use in the keeping up of his image? It is fair to say that an almost universal characteristic of the cults is an insatiable financial appetite in the leadership. They cruelly dangle their followers over the fires of hell as the punishment for not giving large amounts of money to their cause.

The false religions of the world are characterized by lavish temples overlaid with gold and studded with diamonds. Most of them stand in the midst of a sea of poverty that the cults themselves have caused. Their apparent prosperity is nothing more than the shameful result of their cruel exploitation of frightened people who seek their favors with financial gifts. The illustrations are endless. We dare to pray that true Christianity will become increasingly an illustration of the opposite point of view—the *free* grace of Jesus Christ.

We may rejoice in the vast sums of money that have been given by earnest Christians over the years. The result is that local churches, missionary efforts, radio broadcasts, literature ministries, and hundreds of other solid spiritual endeavors have flourished as sincere Christians have poured out their gifts and their earnest prayers. Let us pray, however, that there shall not be within the ranks of true Christianity those who presume on the saints, thinking of people as sources of economic capability rather than eternal souls.

The Root of All Evil

After thinking of these things, we can easily understand why the Bible says that the love of money is the root of all evil. In pursuing money, many a person fulfills the warning of Scripture: "Those who want to get rich fall into temptation and a snare and many foolish and harmful desires which plunge men into ruin and destruction" (1 Timothy 6:9). Yes, Satan himself pays very special attention to the covetous person. When that person achieves some degree of spiritual leadership, he functions especially well as a representative of the satanic kingdom.

These evil functionaries abound in the realm of religion in our time. By way of warning, we do well to remember a principle that will stand us in good stead: *It is an evil thing to promise a physical result that will come from a financial investment in spiritual matters.* Despite the obvious truth of this statement, prosperity, healing, a new house, and answered prayers are still promised to followers if they will just send money.

Recently a woman called our office with a sad account of financial exploitation. Some convincing television speaker presented a proposition to his listeners: "Send me your money and I promise that God will double what you have sent, and will do so within 30 days." Our caller foolishly believed this promise and sent virtually her entire life savings to the promiser on television. Needless to say, the promise was not fulfilled. She has now lost her home and has moved to an apartment in another city. The television preacher operated as if the Bible does not teach the existence of the judgment seat of Christ. To have used a level of Christian leadership in this exploitive fashion is robbery, pure and simple. We must all learn again the lesson that one cannot have faith in what God has *not* promised. It is dishonest to promise predictable external results as a consequence of a financial investment. It is possible that every reader of these pages can think of a financial exploitation scam that has been placed upon him or someone in his circle of acquaintance. Still the practice goes on, and the carnage is truly horrible.

The Results of Exploitation

No one knows how many disillusioned seekers populate our present culture, disenchanted with the church because of promises made that were impossible to fulfill. I personally know of a gentleman who received Christ as a result of the testimony of a certain pastor. At first he rejoiced in the news of eternal life. Within a week, however, the pastor returned to tell the new convert that his decision for Christ would cost him $3200. The point was that the newly converted gentleman received a salary of $32,000 per year, and now that he had come to know the Lord, he owed ten percent to the church!

The requirement that the convert to Christ *must* pay ten percent of his income is unknown to New Testament Scripture. Still, it is practiced by many. While there is nothing wrong with paying ten percent of one's salary to the local church, and God certainly loves a cheerful giver, the notion that the church has somehow obligated a recent convert to a financial commitment is heretical.

The promoter who is interested in financial exploitation will soon conduct his affairs in a fashion condemned by God. James says, "If a man comes into your assembly with a gold ring and dressed in fine clothes, and there also comes in a poor man in dirty clothes, and you pay special attention to the one who is wearing the fine clothes, and say, 'You sit here in a good place,' and you say to the poor man, 'You stand over there, or sit down by my footstool,' have you not made distinctions among yourselves, and become judges with evil motives?" (James 2:2-4). I fear that this would be nearly the last passage in the Bible believed by a cultic promoter. Yet the cults carry on, being sustained by the practice—the love of money—that the Scripture says is the root of every evil. Considering the massive financial programs growing in the world of religion, one does well to consider the contrasts between the Christian and the cultic. There is, or should be, a distinct difference.

STUDY QUESTIONS

1. What gift have Christians been given, according to Romans 6:23?

2. How does that differ from the "wages of sin" in Romans 3:23?

3. What blessings have we received from God, according to Ephesians 1:3-14?

4. In Acts 8:9-24, for what sin was Simon rebuked? Why is that evil?

5. How can something as generous as tithing turn into a cultic practice?

The Outsider As Enemy

Those outside our group are our enemies!

When one announces himself as the true messiah, all others become false and must be put down. Some of the most bitter imprecations in print are the scathing calumny of cultic messiahs upon all who do not believe their views and join their organizations. One sometimes suspects that these leaders are infected with a horrible inferiority complex, pushing them to a neurotic defensiveness. They are for the most part unwilling to appear in public debate or answer questions from perceptive Christian scholars concerning the nature of their faith. Expressing their persecution complex, they denounce all alternative views as being satanic and corrupt.

The contrast of true Christianity is marked. The Bible teaches that there is one Savior, Jesus Christ, and one way of salvation, faith in His finished work on the cross. Within that wonderful circle of faith, however, the Scripture allows for a great diversity of views. Each individual Christian is a believer-priest, and he is related to God as a person.

The Unity of Christians

The apostle Paul, in writing to the Philippians on the subject of Christian unity, said, "Let us therefore, as many as are perfect, have this attitude; and if in anything you have a different attitude, God will reveal that also to you"

(Philippians 3:15). In writing to Timothy, he suggested that his views be considered against the final light of divine understanding. He sharply disagreed with Barnabas over John Mark on one of his missionary journeys (Acts 15:38,39), but this same John Mark was later used of the Holy Spirit to write the gospel of Mark. He was later acknowledged by Paul as a useful Christian worker (2 Timothy 4:11).

Peter claimed that some of Paul's writings were "hard to be understood" (2 Peter 3:16), but recognized Paul as a beloved brother who was writing according to the wisdom that was given unto him. Christ prayed for the very people crucifying Him, saying, "Father, forgive them, for they know not what they do." And while Paul recognized that some rejected him, he also prayed that it would not be laid to their account. "At my first defense no one supported me, but all deserted me; may it not be counted against them" (2 Timothy 4:16).

True Christians are forbidden to judge one another (Romans 14:13). They are given the liberty to be persuaded in their own minds as to how to live unto the Lord (Romans 14:5). They are even told to "not go on passing judgment before the time, but wait until the Lord comes who will both bring to light the things hidden in the darkness and disclose the motives of men's hearts; and then each man's praise will come to him from God" (1 Corinthians 4:5).

The cultic attitude is a fearful contrast. The late Herbert Armstrong declared:

> There is only one work, that is preaching the true gospel of the kingdom of God—the rule and reign of God—to the nations. This is that work. Then those who have their part in this work and are converted must constitute the Church of God! Every other work rejects the message of Jesus Christ or

else rejects His rule through His laws. There is no exception. Yes, this work is the work of the true church of God. All others are satanic counterfeits! It is time we come out from among them and become separate.

The Jehovah's Witnesses have also distributed millions of leaflets announcing:

God will destroy all false religion soon!

God has given the world's religions a long time to prove what they are. Today we see their rotten fruitage all over the earth.

The Bible shows that God's day for accounting is now at hand. For the honor of His own name, which has long been slandered, and for the eternal good of all persons who love righteousness, God must and will act. What will He do?

His inspired Word compares the world empire of false religion to a grossly immoral woman named "Babylon the Great." She is "richly adorned," living in "shameless luxury." In her is found the "blood of all earth's slaughtered." God sentences her to be "burned with fire," completely destroyed. (See Revelation chapters 17 and 18.) This destruction will come from the very political powers that she has dominated for so long. What does this mean for you? [12]

By this they mean that all other religious points of view except that of the Jehovah's Witnesses are condemned. The sincere Christian will conduct himself very carefully when it comes to criticism of others. The often-repeated sense of Scripture is that the work of God is carried on by many individuals, and not one of them can claim that he has a corner on the market so far as divine revelation is concerned.

Christ told His disciples, "I sent you to reap that for which you have not labored; others have labored, and you have entered into their labor" (John 4:38).

We are reminded in Scripture that one is guilty of the most forbidden kind of arrogance when he presumes to judge the activity of his brothers and sisters who labor for the Lord. "Who are you to judge the servant of another?" Paul asks in Romans 14:4. "Why do you regard your brother with contempt?" he continues in verse 10. "For we shall *all* stand before the judgment seat of God" (emphasis added). True laborers for Christ are admonished to "keep the unity of the Spirit in the bond of peace" (Ephesians 4:3). Paul also encourages us to "pursue the things which make for peace and the building up of one another" (Romans 14:19).

Who Is the Enemy?

To a believer, those outside the church are not the enemy—they are victims of the enemy. We are not to hate them; we are to love them into the kingdom of God. Christ set us an example by praying for the very people who were nailing Him to the cross. When a church begins to see those outside it as enemies, you can be sure they have crossed from Christian to cultic.

We are often warned in Scripture to be suspicious of those whose first calling seems to be to produce divisions within the church of Christ. When grievous wolves from the outside enter in, or when from the ranks of Christians there are those who arise "speaking perverse things" (Acts 20:30), there are bound to be those who turn their attention from the things of the Lord toward a new fascination with the provocative words of an aspiring human leader.

Much unsettlement has been caused by those with pretended convictions who demand a hearing and who are often purveyors of a "new discovery of truth." The apostle Paul earnestly exhorted, "Now I urge you, brethren, keep your eye on those who cause dissensions and hindrances contrary to the teaching which you learned, and turn away from them. For such men are slaves, not of our Lord Christ but of their own appetites; and by their smooth and flattering speech they deceive the hearts of the unsuspecting" (Romans 16:17,18).

Be wary of those who seek to divide or destroy. Stay away from those who preach hate and hostility. Instead, follow the command of our Lord, who, while speaking to the crowds from the mountainside, said, "Love your enemies, and pray for those who persecute you in order that you may be sons of your Father who is in heaven" (Matthew 5:44,45).

STUDY QUESTIONS

1. How are Christians to view non-Christians?

2. How does that differ from the way cult members often view outsiders?

3. What example are we to set, according to 1 Peter 2:12?

4. What warning does Paul offer in Romans 14:12-18?

5. When have you seen Christians denounced?

All Things to All People

We must become all things to all people!

This worthy goal, reflecting a statement of principle by the apostle Paul in 1 Corinthians 9:22, ought to be adopted by every Christian. The witness for Christ must find a way to establish contact with people who come from different cultural, religious, and racial backgrounds. The first problem for anyone who would reach others for Christ is to find a way to minister the eternal truth of the Word of God in language that can move across wars of culture and prejudice. The Christian communicator must find appropriate ways to "become as" the people to whom he ministers.

Within this total context, however, is a line beyond which we must not move. The loving concern for spiritual accommodation can be pressed to the point where it compromises the gospel of Christ, sometimes beyond recognition. This involves one in a grievous sin called syncretism.

Syncretism describes the attempt to gather together what some would call "the best qualities" of various religious points of view in order to create a new and acceptable faith. It is the attempt to synchronize the otherwise diverse religious elements currently believed by people to make a new religion attractive. The definition of *syncretism* from a religious point of view is "the process of growth through coalescence of different forms of faith and worship or through accretions of tenets, rights, etc., from those religions which are being superseded."

Syncretism is a favorite cultic device. Both the older and the emergent cults, almost without exception, have accommodated themselves to existing religious points of view, incorporating older doctrines into their systems of faith along with new and creative heresies. Few cults of our time present much that is really new in the world of religion. Almost invariably they are a rehash of existing concepts, both orthodox and heretical. They present warmed-over elements of Protestantism, Catholicism, paganism, pantheism, idolatry, and local fetishes.

What Will You Buy?

One can almost imagine a cult promoter looking at a city or a country and asking himself, "What will these people buy?" As he reflects on the situation, trying to determine the most palatable combination of philosophical ideas, he wonders, "What are their hopes, dreams, prejudices, and hang-ups? And how can I give them a religious view they will support?" The cult promoter is not so foolish as to come on the scene talking initially about the Great Pumpkin or green men from Mars. He talks about Christ, the Bible, the Holy Spirit, miracles, and other elements of the Christian revelation. The untutored listener is impressed, often believing this person to be a Christian who is just a little wiser than most.

Then comes the hook. The cult organizer subtly introduces his theological non sequitur. He may, like the "Process Church," suggest that Lucifer is not really an enemy of God but one of His better friends. He may, like Mary Baker Eddy, suggest that personal benefit comes not from the gracious hand of God, but from the proper state of mind. It happens in a hundred ways and in a thousand places as the wolf in sheep's clothing presents his composite religious views to deceive the unwary.

It happens in our major cities. Los Angeles, for instance, is the great boiling pot of new religions. Its sacred temples, golden altars, religious sciences, midnight seances, healing potions, miraculous handkerchiefs, pyramid power, and "spiritual gospel of relativity" all testify to the spiritual vulnerability of this and other metropolitan areas. Sensing some new, exploitative possibilities, the cultist glues together a bewildering array of religious components, knowing that some of these will strike a chord of response. He reaches into every conceivable human interest, promising the benefits of transcendental meditation, psycho-cybernetics, spiritual rationalization, and mental science. Incorporating these in the same package with a few theological terms, he is off and running with another cult.

Syncretism and Paganism

A similar thing happens on the mission fields of the world. Missionaries, some of them with only parachurch backgrounds, arrive in an area already steeped in religion. Animism, ancestor worship, religious paganism, or raw heathenism are flourishing. Hoping to minimize the offense of their Christianity, the missionaries accommodate themselves to the local religious climate. Sometimes the resulting religion brings together a regional god, an animal sacrifice, the Virgin Mary, and Jesus Christ all in the same system. Syncretism on mission fields is becoming one of the scandals of the religious world. *A syncretistic religion is not Christianity at all; it is a cult!*

The cults have been syncretists for a long time. Mary Baker Eddy is an illustration of this. Impressed with a certain faith healer, P.P. Quimby, a semispiritualist, Eddy's imagination was triggered as to ways of merging his peculiar

views with the Bible. Quimby himself started with old-fash-
ioned mesmerism and soon developed his own version of
this mental healing gimmick. Eddy simply added her own
twists and created a syncretistic cult.

The Worldwide Church of God is another illustration of
syncretism. The Armstrong followers picked up a few ideas
from the Seventh-day Adventists and tied them with British
Israelism. These, thrown together with a few extra ideas
about diet, health, and the messianic leadership of Armstrong, produced a new and attractive religious combination. The whole mess, energized by strong religious
promotion, produced a religion that eventually took in a
million dollars every week in America. Praise God the new
leaders of that group have recognized their errors and
chosen to return to orthodoxy.

Evangelical Christians look with understandable astonishment at such syncretistic cults. We do well to remember,
however, that syncretism can be a very subtle, creeping
heresy, moving into many unexpected places. We hear talk
in churches today that may open the door to acceptance of
a religious potpourri that is something other than Christianity. A Christian theologian said at a recent conference
that the great need in the world today is for the message of
Christianity to become "a full-orbed gospel for the whole
man." Eloquent sentences such as this sound beautiful, but
they can become an open door to unbiblical doctrine. When
anybody's gospel becomes more "full-orbed" than the
gospel which is very carefully stated in the Word of God,
that "gospel" ceases to be the gospel at all.

What Is the Gospel?

The gospel is the good news of salvation in Christ, and
it is very categorically defined in the Word of God. When

writing to the Corinthian church, which was already infected with heresy, the apostle Paul noted,

> Now I make known to you, brethren, the gospel which I preached to you, which also you received, in which also you stand, by which also you are saved, if you hold fast the word which I preached to you, unless you believed in vain. For I delivered to you as of first importance what I also received, that Christ died for our sins according to the Scriptures, and that He was buried, and that He was raised on the third day according to the Scriptures (1 Corinthians 15:1-4).

It is clear from this definition of the gospel that there is no special "full-orbed gospel for the whole man." That is, the gospel does not of itself promise to change the social structure, the political climate, or the physical environment of those who, even after exercising faith in Christ, live in the midst of a fallen world. When the gospel gets wider or more inclusive than Paul's definition in this passage it ceases to be the gospel and becomes merely a set of unattainable religious promises.

There are still other forms of subtle syncretism. Many groups of Christians today rejoice in the gospel *plus* a wonderful religious heritage. The sacred traditions of many religions have been a significant source of stability as they guide their way through the new problems of this current generation. "Our fathers" have bequeathed to many of us a sacred trust in the teachings of Scripture that has stood us in good stead during our moments of spiritual vertigo.

Looking to the past, however, can produce subtle deceptions in our Christian thinking. Surely what the church needs today is not so much the "faith of our fathers," but the faith of Jesus Christ as expressed in the changeless Scriptures of the New Testament. Heritage can become a dangerous element in the thinking of Christians because it is almost always applied to a human tradition which is only partially biblical. Great time-honored religious traditions are ordinarily formed to protect by custom certain theological propositions that are unvoiced in the Word of God. "Our sacred heritage" is more often than not a melodramatic expression used to call for loyalty to someone else beside Jesus Christ and something else beside the truth of Scripture.

The Call to a Social Gospel

Another syncretistic tendency has been the movement of the great denominations to include "the imperative of social action" in their preaching of the gospel. This has been true to the extent that they have been legitimately accused of preaching a social gospel. Now many evangelical Christians are speaking about "the social implications of the gospel in our time." Soon the word *implications* changes to the word *responsibilities*. It is but a short step to move from here to the use of the word *imperatives*.

When asked, "What are the social implications of the gospel?" many an earnest evangelical begins to speak swelling words of wisdom that are simply impossible to understand. Many sound as if they had learned their theology in a sociology class and have yet to put $10 under their indigent neighbor's sugar bowl in the name of Jesus Christ. The gospel may indeed have social implications (fewer, I think, than are commonly touted), but this is another, infinitely less important subject than the death of Jesus Christ on the cross and His glorious resurrection. The one produces eternal salvation; the other produces endless discussion.

The point is that Christians need an adequate understanding of Christian doctrine to discern the difference between what the gospel *is* and what the gospel *implies*.

We need to comprehend anew that which is absolute about the revelation of Jesus Christ and those things which are relative in decreasing steps of importance. Political change, physical healing, peace marching, temperance activities, clothing styles—the list is endless, and all are interesting subjects for Christian discussion. They are not, however, to be put in the same class with the finished work of Jesus Christ on the cross by which He takes away the sins of the world.

The Impact of the Gospel

Christianity has had a very interesting past. We may talk about the church of Christ moving "like a mighty army" from its early beginnings in the city of Jerusalem, to the place where it has swept across the far reaches of western civilization. The fact of the matter is that it hasn't been quite like that. A high percentage of the countries that have been moved by the gospel of Jesus Christ in other times are now custodians of a dead religion that still masquerades under the name Christianity. The horizon of practically every city in western civilization is dotted with the steeples of buildings called "churches," which are but grim, spectral monuments of a past life that is now long gone.

Europe resembles a vast cemetery of the Christian religion with only grave markers left to show for what once was a vital faith. Little of Christianity remains in the countries of its origin. The record seems to show that our faith has prospered best in new, pioneer situations on the cutting edge of civilization as it has moved from east to west. As churches grew older, they seem to have given themselves to the spirit of accommodation while forgetting their heavenly calling. They set up ecumenical movements, national conferences of Christians and Jews, and endless other movements to make their situation more legitimate. They opted for political change and social action and have worked with sincerity to redress the grievances of the oppressed within society. Time, money, and irreplaceable human energy went into these worthy causes—and salvation from sin seemed pale by comparison.

What was the consequence? In country after country the gospel of Jesus Christ has been forgotten. Churches died and never knew it. The glory and the blessing of God departed, and preoccupied religionists were too blind to sense that their candlestick had been removed. Syncretism, the attempt to synchronize the gospel of Christ with a god-less world, is a deadly virus from which almost no institution recovers. This virus can infect us all and, becoming a plague, can carry us all away. When the Son of Man is come, will He find the Christian faith on the earth?

STUDY QUESTIONS

1. What is *syncretism?*

2. How do cults try to synchronize their beliefs and actions?

3. What danger is there for Christians to do so?

4. Cults could never attract people if they openly declared they believed in "spaceships hidden behind comets that will take us to another world." How do they attract people?

5. Imagine a friend said to you, "Christians have to be involved in social ministry or they are not fulfilling the command of God. We need to be feeding the hungry, housing the homeless, and freeing the oppressed. Without that, our faith doesn't prove itself." How would you reply?

What Shall We Do?

Like a river glorious is the church of God. . . .

It is surely the case that we are seeing a spawning of satanic cults in a measure almost beyond comprehension. Some of the old cults are splitting into several new varieties, and new cults are beginning with every week that passes. Clever individuals with a smattering of religious knowledge are emboldened by their own pride and motivated by Satan to press for their own piece of influence in today's religious scene.

In the face of all of this, concerned people are asking as never before what they can do to protect themselves and their loved ones from these terrible, subversive religious influences. Surely the course of action that we who would be true to Christ must take includes the following activities and directions of study:

1. *Understand Christian doctrine:* The chief reason for the success of cults is the spiritual naïveté on the part of people. Far too many Christians are content with a superficial knowledge of the Word of God, thinking themselves spiritually intelligent. Nothing could be further from the truth! The Christian must give himself to a detailed study of Scripture and understand the Bible from a doctrinal point of view. He should have valid biblical information that answers questions such as: Who is God? What is man? What is sin? What do we mean by biblical inspiration?

We live in a time when doctrine has been played down in favor of Christian experience. This is the most foolish course imaginable because experience has little or nothing to do with Christian truth. Our experiences are merely human. They are the responses of our nervous system to spiritual truth or error that impinges on our minds and hearts. The evangelical leader who says, "We do not need more doctrine, but more experience" should rethink his theology. He is playing into the hands of the cultic wolves who prowl on the edges of the flock. The simple lambs who pursue additional experiences may get their titillation from the big, bad, but seemingly friendly wolf.

2. *Separate from spiritual subversion:* The apostle Paul carefully warned the believers at Ephesus to "not participate in the unfruitful deeds of darkness, but instead even expose them" (Ephesians 5:11). Many people ask whether they should attend meetings of cultic religious organizations and give themselves to an extensive reading of subversive religious literature so they will know what they're fighting. With rare exceptions, the answer to this question is *no,* a thousand times no!

An inquiry into the nuances of false doctrine is an endless pursuit. Few people have the time or the available energy to know all that can be known about the myriad of false religious philosophies of our time. It is not true that we cannot speak critically of false doctrine unless we have read everything that the leadership of these cults has to say. One only has to eat a good steak to realize that the contents of a thousand garbage cans are simply beneath his standards.

There are foolish Christians who are too inquisitive and who ought to heed the advice of one of Stuart Hamblin's songs, "Why should I fool with calico, when I have silk at home?" The statement that says, "You cannot know what it is until you have tried it" is a satanic doctrine—and it is the very one that he used to subvert Eve and bring the terrible cancer of sin into all the world.

3. *Refuse profane points of view:* These are the very words with which Paul advised Timothy in 1 Timothy 4:7. The apostle was aware that the world would be filled with spiritual exhibitionists and religious lunatics who would for hours and even days tie up the time and energy of anyone willing to listen to them. We live in a time in which stories come to us about pictures of Christ in the clouds, resurrections in remote jungle areas, preachers in some obscure town with a new and unheard of doctrine, and endless additional tales.

Christians are enjoined not to give themselves to these things, but rather to follow the good advice extended to Timothy: "Give attention to the public reading of Scripture, to exhortation and teaching" (1 Timothy 4:13). Further, we are called upon to "take pains with these things; be absorbed in them, so that your progress may be evident to all" (1 Timothy 4:15).

It is clear that the Christian must not float through life on the wave of some existential euphoria. Rather, the Scripture commands again and again that he must be careful, take heed, watch, and remember. He is called upon to be very sober because his satanic adversary continues to go about seeking whom he may devour (see 1 Peter 5:8).

4. *Do not encourage cultic practitioners:* The Christian is supposed to be loving in his attitude toward people, but he must also face the hard truth that many deceivers have come into the world who do not believe the gospel of Jesus Christ and are, in fact, enemies of the Lord. They are antichrists. Concerning these, he is admonished to be very careful and not to risk his spiritual stability by allowing himself to be deceived.

The apostle John wrote: "Anyone who goes too far and does not abide in the teaching of Christ, does not have God; the one who abides in the teaching, he has both the Father and the Son. If anyone comes to you and does not bring this teaching, do not receive him into your house, and do not give him a greeting; for the one who gives him a greeting participates in his evil deeds" (2 John 9-11). This is the hard but necessary course of action for one who would protect himself and his family from spiritual danger.

5. *Be willing to contend for the faith:* Scripture calls upon us to earnestly contend for the faith, which means to be willing to defend the truth of the gospel in the face of satanic adversaries (see Jude 3). We have illustrations in Scripture that this sometimes means coming to a point of contention with friends and associates. The apostle Paul was surely a beloved friend of the apostle Peter, but he said, "When Cephas came to Antioch, I opposed him to his face, because he stood condemned" (Galatians 2:11). In this case, Peter was guilty of doctrinal error and was cooperating with the Judaizers who were subverting the people of Galatia into heresy.

Indeed Jesus Christ Himself had on one occasion to turn to His beloved friend Peter and say, "Get behind Me, Satan" (Matthew 16:23). The true servant of Jesus Christ must be careful that his friendship with the Lord is the association that is absolute. By comparison, all human associations are relative. The first principle of the universe is truth, and it must be defended even at the cost of our lives. Surely the apostle Paul was serious when he named us all as soldiers of the cross and gave us a detailed list of the armor that we should wear in order to function properly as contenders for the faith (see Ephesians 6:10-20).

Our spiritual sentiments (and this is the most sentimental age in the history of the church) would lead us many times to feel that contention for the faith of the gospel is somehow unspiritual or undignified. *Nothing could be further from the truth.* The analogy of the Christian being a soldier of the cross is one that is repeated many times in Holy Scripture. The world is described as a battleground, and the essential struggle on that field of conquest is the struggle between truth and untruth. We are called to stand for truth in a world that embraces lies.

STUDY QUESTIONS

1. Give yourself a theology quiz: If someone asked you to explain God, sin, or biblical inspiration, what would you say?

2. What is the meaning of Ephesians 5:11?

3. What specific instruction does Paul offer Timothy in 1 Timothy 4:6-16? Which of these things do you need to work on?

4. In practical terms, how are we to put into effect 2 John 9-11?

5. When are you given an opportunity to contend for the faith?

From Christian to Cultic

My hope is built on nothing less than Jesus'
blood and righteousness.

There is a very noticeable drift in today's religious scene
that affects churches, Christian organizations, individuals,
publishing companies, and most of the entities that are a
part of Christian activities. Many comments could be said
about its interesting nuances, but the best way to describe
most of the "drift" is to say that it represents a move from
Christian to cultic. There are thousands of cults in the
United States and the world today, many of them having
once been classified as legitimate Christian religious activities. How does this happen, and how may it be discerned?
We move from Christian to cultic when...

1. *We attempt to make visible what God has made*
invisible.

Describing Christian reality the Bible says, "While we
look not at the things which are seen, but at the things
which are not seen; for the things which are seen are temporal, but the things which are not seen are eternal" (2 Corinthians 4:18). The essence of Christianity is unseen. It is
resident in Jesus Christ, who has not yet come from heaven
for His own. People, however, thirst for things that can be
seen with the eyes. Many are unwilling to settle for an invisible faith. This desire for visible things, as we have noted

earlier, is called *phenomenalism*. Sensing this desire, many forms of religion have set up altars, crosses, candles, stained glass, liturgies, vestments, sacristies, and other forms of visible tokens in order to fill the eyes of people with that religious practice. The more a religion is visible, the less it represents the eternal truth of the invisible God.

2. When we sell for money what God has given for free.

One of the great things about the gospel is that it comes to us on a basis that is absolutely free. In order to be saved, there is nothing to buy, nothing to pay for, nothing to give. We are invited to believe in Jesus Christ and receive the totally *free gift* of salvation. The lustful religionist, however, senses that there is profit to be made. Consequently, he sets up a religion that demands payment for salvation. This payment is called by many things: dedication, tithing, indulgences, and a score of other names. He is selling the wonderful gift of salvation and is thereby guilty of criminal theological negligence—a great sin.

3. When we make complicated what God has made simple.

It is true that the Bible is theologically complicated, but the way of salvation is not. The way of salvation says, "Believe on the Lord Jesus Christ and you will be saved." That simple path from sin to righteousness is filled by today's modern religious leaders with stumbling blocks, steppingstones, briars, twists, turns, and eternal tantalizers to take the next step. Salvation that becomes complicated is cultic rather than Christian.

4. When we enslave those whom God has made free.

To every Christian the Bible says, "It was for freedom that Christ set us free; therefore, keep standing firm and do not be subject again to a yoke of slavery" (Galatians 5:1).

Subjugating the saints is one of the favorite occupations of the leaders of our time. As a consequence of this nefarious activity, many humble Christians are pitiful slaves to a religious system when they should be God's free children. Again, this is the doctrine of the Nicolaitans, which God hates.

5. When we demand works for those things that God gives by grace.

The Scripture says, "But if it is by grace, it is no longer on the basis of works, otherwise grace is no longer grace" (Romans 11:6). Salvation, in the first place, is by grace. And on all subsequent occasions, God deals with us by grace as well, in this we may rejoice. The apostle Paul said, "But by the grace of God I am what I am" (1 Corinthians 15:10). To demand works for the things God gives away freely is enslaving and cultic.

6. When we substitute human leaders for our blessed Lord.

This is a gross violation of the command of Christ: "But do not be called Rabbi; for One is your Teacher, and you are all brothers. And do not call anyone on earth your father; for One is your Father, He who is in heaven" (Matthew 23:8,9). The Scripture gives no such power to human leaders as is arrogated to themselves by themselves in religious circles of our time.

There can be many other evidences that a church, a denomination, or a Christian individual is moving from Christian to cultic. The beliefs and signs we've covered are a beginning, and they are presented in the earnest hope they will help stem the drift from the true Christian faith into many of the organized heresies that are coming upon us.

Is My Church a Cult?

More people today than in all of history are hearing the gospel and are aware of the existence of Christianity and its mounting impact upon society. Christ made a prediction we should remember. He told us that the wheat, the maturing harvest, would grow tall as we move toward the end of the age. But He also told us that an alien seed sown by "an enemy" would produce tares that would grow along with the wheat. We rejoice in the wheat that is maturing into the harvest. Along with that rejoicing, however, we must be sober and vigilant, aware of the tares that now grow up in our midst (see Matthew 13:24-30).

We ought not be surprised at the inauthentic and false versions of Christianity that are now growing up. The apostle Paul warned the elders of the Ephesian church, saying, "I know that after my departure savage wolves will come in among you, not sparing the flock; and from among your own selves men will arise, speaking perverse things, to draw away the disciples after them. Therefore be on the alert, remembering that night and day for a period of three years I did not cease to admonish each one with tears" (Acts 20:29-31). Paul preached the gospel most positively. He also delivered a tearful warning on the negative, subversive influences which would come upon the church as it moved through its history.

Thus we are warned that many churches and religious institutions would move from the true to the false. Starting out as authentic, spiritual entities, they would become cultic rather than Christian. Believers therefore do well to set up a clinic for the early detection of spiritual deviation. Just as early detection of physical disease can initiate therapy that may preserve life, early detection of spiritual disease can be a preserver of the spiritual life of a church or institution.

The revival for which many plead today had better be a revival of attention to sound doctrine. Other forms of revival will do far more harm than good.

The Christian does well to face the question, "Is the Christian organization of which I am a part moving from Christian to cultic?" In other words, "Is my church staying with the true faith or straying toward becoming a cult?" To the perceptive mind, the early symptoms of spiritual disease are not difficult to detect. Cultic tendencies can easily be noticed by asking some relatively simple questions concerning one's church or Christian institution.

Has my church begun to teach things that are not in the Bible?

If the first and foremost mark of a cult is extrabiblical revelation, then we had better make sure the teaching we hear comes straight from the Scripture. Most churches start with a commitment to biblical inerrancy and authority, and they initially prosper because the pulpit is given to the preaching of the Word. "Thus says the Lord" is an oft-repeated expression from the lips of the preacher. Soon, however, a subtle change takes place. Talk begins to arise from the people of such things as "our tradition" or "our heritage." Eventually a mere practice becomes a doctrine. Then a whole set of doctrines begins to emerge which are unknown to Scripture, so that the Word is supplanted by human formulas.

Christ spoke about such a development when He said, "But in vain do they worship me, teaching as doctrines the precepts of men" (Mark 7:7). Such people are hypocrites, appearing "spiritual," but all the time committing the sin of perverting the Scriptures. Christians could now use a touch of sanctified cynicism, asking often, "Does the Bible really teach that?"

Is the leader becoming absolute and indispensable?

Churches and religious institutions, of course, need leaders, and rules are given regarding the qualities of these leaders. As leaders develop capability, however, they are often tempted to put themselves into the place of Christ. So it is that now some churches hear from the leader the expression, *"I* forgive your sins." The leader may even think of himself as an intermediary, a conduit to God. He may then imply that there is something special about his prayers or his thinking. Especially beware if he promises that he will bring special prayers for you "at Calvary" or "at the Mount of Olives" or "in the desert." Such a person forgets that "there is one God, and one mediator also between God and men, the man Christ Jesus, who gave Himself as a ransom for all" (1 Timothy 2:5,6). The Bible teaches that Christ alone is our high priest. It then announces the priesthood of every believer. Messianic leaders and intermediaries are cultic. So are all brokers of divine blessing.

Are "things" becoming holy?

In the Old Testament, there were "sacred things" such as the tabernacle, the temple, the altar, the holy of holies, and the ark of the covenant. These holy implements were to be held in awe and handled by the rules which divine law prescribed. Within New Testament Christianity, however, there are no such holy instruments. Nevertheless, people devoid of spiritual discernment continue to invest worldly things with a sense of the divine dwelling in them. So it is that articles, pieces of metal, wood, or plastic are called "sacred crosses," "altars," "sacred desks," "sacristies"—and the list goes on. These things ought not to be. To imbue that sort of power into human objects is cultic.

But people continue to do so. Why? The answer is simple: They have promotional value. Organizers of religions know that awe can be produced, loyalty evoked, money raised, and obedience guaranteed if people are led to believe there is a certain magic about physical things. There is not. *No article that we can see, feel, or touch is sacred.* No human instrument is an entity in which the divine is present. The apostle Paul said, "We look not at the things which are seen, but at the things which are not seen; for the things which are seen are temporal, but the things which are not seen are eternal" (2 Corinthians 4:18).

Nevertheless, the promotional value of pot-metal religious symbols, pieces of the cross, luminous prayer reminders, or sand from the Holy Land continues. By these the unprincipled exploit the unwary. Both are sadly deceived. The religion that attempts to make visible what God has made invisible is moving from Christian to cultic.

Is clothing sacred?

In many religious fellowships it is customary for robes to be worn, often by the pastor, the choir, the baptismal candidates, and others. Such a practice is neither advocated nor discouraged in Scripture, so in this a person can be persuaded in his own mind what is right. But remember, uniformity tends to be cultic, while diversity is Christian.

Beware, however, of the greater danger. Religious clothing always means that the wearer wants us to assume something about himself and impute some special quality. Robes have a way of becoming "vestments." How often the simple attire takes to itself stripes, collars, crosses, colors, and emblems which signify the rank or station of the wearer. There are worship leaders who must wear five or six layers of "sacred garments" in order to fulfill a long-standing traditional prescription. This is an indication that the leader is becoming presumptuous and messianic. The very word *vestment* implies that apparel is vested with a sacred significance it does not possess of itself. To the degree that this arrogation is allowed to continue, the wearer and his church are moving from Christian to cultic.

Is Christ being redefined?

A very critical mark of cults is that they preach a defective Christology. Jesus Christ is the Son of God, the Son of Man, and the Savior of mankind. He came, He said, "To seek and to save that which is lost" (Luke 19:10). Many a church and denomination began with blessing, believing the truth about Jesus Christ. Down through the years, however, attitudes have a way of changing. Christ is redefined in terms of His person and His mission. Almost all cults deny the deity of Christ. Some deny His humanity, and many deny His historic authenticity. Confusing His purpose, many are tempted when beholding poverty to claim that the primary mission of Christ was that He came to be an economic liberator, a messiah of the poor. Christ is redefined, and His mission restated to serve a cause which is incidental, but made a *cause célèbre* by the modern radical.

Others, believing that man is essentially good but immature, define Christ as merely "our example," like an older brother who shows us the way. This half-truth becomes a whole lie, and Christ is denied His deity and His role as Savior. The church or the religious movement that defines Christ in a way other than "Son of the living God and Savior of the world" is becoming a cult. So it is that in many churches today Christ is being represented as a loving sentimentalist, a militant revolutionary, or a political messiah, rather than the Savior and judge of history. Such denominations are not above sponsoring a new translation of the Bible to bolster their views.

Is money so important that it overshadows all else?

Finally, a Christian should ask himself if money has taken precedence over the Lord in his church. All Christian efforts must have money. The pastors and teachers live on the support of the people of God. Christians are, therefore, enjoined to give to support the work of Christ.

It is easy, however, for unscrupulous leaders to exploit the willingness of Christians to give. If the church or the cause becomes so big and costly that it must resort to ruthless promotion in order to survive, it is cultic. Christ spoke of this with some of His most severe condemnation: "Woe to you, scribes and Pharisees, hypocrites, because you devour widows' houses, even while for a pretense you make long prayers; therefore you shall receive greater condemnation" (Matthew 23:14). How many vulnerable widows and widowers, infirm and overly trusting, have been impoverished by the impassioned promotion of the religious charlatans in our time? Peter gives us a frightening description of false teachers, saying, "In their greed they will exploit you with false words; their judgment from long ago is not idle, and their destruction is not asleep" (2 Peter 2:3). In the lecherous eyes of the cultic promoter, people are seen not as children of God, but as potential sources of money. A church marked by financial exploitation is well on the way toward becoming a cult.

Please bear in mind that I am not only speaking of "those other people"—the bizarre, malicious, religious degenerates who are obviously and publicly corrupt. The danger is not merely from those given to public lechery and obvious lying manipulation. The danger can come closer to home. The subtle departure from truth and honor can come to the known denomination, the trusted church, the gentle pastor, and the familiar seminary. We are not often corrupted by salivating monsters who are obviously repulsive.

No, the worst corruption is that slow-acting poison that is introduced into our minds by those we trust, whose names we know, and whom we revere. Paul warned that "of your own selves shall men arise, speaking perverse things."

Few churches have the courage to refuse ordination to one of their own sons who has come to disbelieve the Scriptures. Few would accuse those they love of spiritual defection, even though "faithful are the wounds of a friend." For want of this courage, many churches are drifting on the warm currents from truth to falsehood, from facts to fantasy, from biblical truth to false academics. In short, they are moving from Christian to cultic.

Concerning these things, today's church has all-too-few leaders who will lift a voice of warning. For want of the courageous truth, the religious establishment of our day often settles for comforting, plausible lies. Too many Christians prefer to be flattered by those who would exploit them, rather than be constructively corrected by those who love and care.

How shall we avoid this? Be vigilant! Remember that communion is Christian, but communes are cultic. Prayer is biblical, but incantation is cultic. Exposition is Scriptural, vain repetition is not. Travel is enlightening, pilgrimages are cultic. Chapels, yes; shrines, no. Humility, certainly; obeisance, never except before God. Inspiration is Christian; asceticism is cultic. Understanding is Christian; "hocus-pocus" is cultic. Healing, perhaps; healers, no. Miracles, rarely; miracle workers, run away. Hope is Christian; predictions are cultic. Confession is biblical; public confession is worrisome. "I have sinned" is contrition; "We have sinned" is suspicious. A church that has begun to slide away from the former and toward the latter has begun a long decline.

STUDY QUESTIONS

1. Read 2 Corinthians 4:18. What is wrong with attempting to make visible what God has made invisible?

2. When have you seen people making a profit on what God has offered for free?

3. In Acts 16:30 the Philippian jailer cries out, "What must I do to be saved?" How did the apostle Paul answer him? What other answers have you seen or heard proclaimed in our culture?

4. What command does Paul give us in Galatians 5:1? Why is it important?

5. What warning does the Lord have for us in Matthew 23:8,9? How have several cults ignored this warning?

Speaking the Truth

Speak the truth in love!

A disabled airplane is a dangerous vehicle. When an engine is on fire, the pilot or passenger would be foolish to call up thoughts of loyalty or tradition as a reason why he should be consumed in the crash. In the same way, too many Christians have stayed in too many apostate institutions because "this is where my father was baptized" or "Grandma is buried in the cemetery out back." What are churches and Christian institutions for? They are here to proclaim the Word of God and the testimony of Jesus Christ, not to sustain the traditions of man. When they cease to promote Christ, they cease to be Christian—no matter how beautiful the stained glass or how high the steeple.

Betrayal of Jesus Christ or denial of the Word of God must never be rationalized in the name of loyalty to anything or anyone. The disciple of such a program who stays too long tends to become further enmeshed in an evil program to the point where he no longer can escape. Then, through rationalization and self-justification, he risks losing his own equilibrium—indeed his own sanity.

The cities and countrysides of our world are sprinkled with cold, spectral, mausoleum-type buildings—the echoing remains of a former spiritual reality, of past workings of the Lord. These buildings are, in many cases, still attended by ghostly people who are the diehard loyalists to a cause long separated from the presence of God and the working of the Holy Spirit. If believers had departed these institutions in sufficient numbers while there still was time, that departure might have been just the spiritual corrective that was needed. For want of that spiritual corrective, many of today's movements may be gaining undeserved strength to work unprecedented carnage in the lives of many.

Witnessing to a Cultist

At some point we will all cross paths with people who have been influenced by the cults. Knowing what to say and how to say it may mean the difference of eternity for those misguided souls. Imagine you are sitting at home one evening when a mysterious stranger comes knocking at your door. Or you may meet him at a shopping center, or an airport, perhaps even at the door of your church or even in your Sunday school class. Wherever it may be, a religious promoter will probably cross your pathway sometime this year.

He or she will be warm, personable, and communicative. The cultist will compliment you on your appearance and perhaps your spiritual perception. There will be talk about "the marvelous potential that you face in life" or "the beautiful fulfillment available to you if you will let me share a remarkable new discovery." At that point, it is time to listen very carefully. Promoters of new and strange religions are moving upon our society with greater activity than ever before. In all probability, they will be well-dressed, carry beautiful literature, and spin a beguiling story for anyone willing to listen. Some of the most vocal and earnest witnessing being done today is by representatives of cults. Quite obviously they are too often successful.

Cults have gained thousands of converts and millions of dollars in contributions in recent years, and they have distributed tons of literature. On radio and television they have achieved unprecedented visibility. The result is that there are more than 3,000 religious cults, with more than five *million* members in America alone. This estimate is conservative, considering the religious organizations that have moved from Christian to cultic and the all-too-common spiritual defection of many. Still, there are millions of troubled spirits moving into the fatal embrace of cults. They need more than ever to hear a witness to the truth of Christ.

And that is the problem. Concerned Christians are asking, "How can I be an effective witness with someone who is enamored with a cult leader, whose mind is apparently closed to the true gospel of Christ?" A cult is an organized heresy; its false views capture a person and become a disease in his intellectual and emotional structure. Rescuing a cultic slave from the depths of spiritual subversion is a difficult task.

But it is possible. Scripture suggests that God may give a person repentance unto the acknowledging of the truth. He may recover from the snare of the devil. Spiritual recovery is possible, but it's not inevitable. There are several principles faithful Christian witnesses should keep in mind.

1. *Pray.*

Keep in mind that the cultist may be under satanic influence. Witnessing to a member of a cult takes great care and a large measure of spiritual power. Pray earnestly and carefully weigh every word, asking God to turn it into spiritual dynamite. It is difficult enough to reach a spiritually neutral person; how much more difficult to touch the mind of one captured by Satan. Prayer is imperative to be a good witness to the cultist.

2. *Know your Bible.*

Witnessing to a cultist will often take the form of spiritual rebuttal. The apostle Paul tells Christians that they must "reprove, rebuke, exhort, with great patience and instruction" (2 Timothy 4:2). A mind that has been made captive by a satanic lie is not open to "sweet reasonableness"—it frequently needs reproof and rebuke. Don't shun sharp and pointed statements. A believer who has studied his Bible, knows his doctrine, and can find or recite pertinent passages will be prepared to discuss his faith with a cultist.

3. Take the initiative.

Christians often ask, "How do I start? How do I open the conversation so that I can talk about Christ?" Almost always the cultic promoter will aggressively seize the initiative and attempt to do most of the talking. A perceptive Christian can respond in kind, often with a sharp word of spiritual correction. We must have a ready knowledge of the Word of God and be ready to respond immediately to the demands of a spiritual discussion. A loving but gently forceful witness for Christ often surprises a cultist. At airports I often step into a situation where a cultic promoter is attempting to convert a traveler. "Look," I'll say to the traveler, "this person is a satanic religionist. He is talking about a cult. Don't take his literature, and don't give him any money. You're a Christian, and Christians know better than that!" (Using the phrase "you're a Christian" has led to many opportunities to explain what being a Christian really means!) Cults not only need an active witness, they need to be confronted. We Christians are too often reticent in our witness for Christ. Assert a word of correction to a cultic promoter.

4. Stay with Scripture.

As you talk, stay close to the Word of God. Many cultists are well-versed in philosophy, and most are especially adept at endless discussion. Like the woman at the well, they can talk endlessly about where we are supposed to worship and what truth is. Such discussions are usually profitless (notice Christ's answer to the woman's pseudo-spiritual discussion was to skip over her pointless arguing in order to state His point).

Don't involve yourself in irrelevant religious discussions. Stay close to Scripture. Quote its teaching on sin, righteousness, the person of Christ, the work of the cross, and the nature of salvation. An aspiring Christian witness, without good command of the Bible, is almost certain to end up second best in an animated discussion with a cultist. The rise of the cults and their remarkable (but warped) knowledge of Scripture should lead many of us back to intense, personal Bible study.

5. *Tell your story.*

Give your testimony for Christ. Tell the cultist how you met the Lord. Many cult members are religious seekers who can be deeply moved by an earnest Christian telling what the Lord has done for him or her. In the depths of his heart, the cultist is still seeking reality and can often be reached by the sincere, heartfelt testimony of a true Christian. Cults are good at producing a pseudo-experience, but devotees are still looking for the real thing.

Warnings to Christians

Remember: *Don't go beyond your depth.* It is unwise to pretend to know something. Find a counselor, pastor, theologian, or spiritual advisor to help answer questions you cannot. Be candid with people. Admitting "I don't know the answer, but I can certainly find out for you," reveals your honesty and can lead to greater dialogue.[13]

A second reminder is this: *Don't give the cultist any money.* One mark of a false teacher is his attempt to make merchandise of you. Representatives of some cults raise hundreds of dollars a day from unsuspecting people who buy books or make contributions to "Christian camps," "counseling centers," or "ministries" of one sort or another. The cultist may pretend to be impressed or even swayed by your arguments, gaining your interest—and then he will ask for money. Don't do it! Keep in mind the warning of the apostle John, who tells us:

> For many deceivers have gone out into the world, those who do not acknowledge Jesus Christ as coming in the flesh. This is the deceiver and the antichrist. Watch yourselves, that you might not lose what we have accomplished, but that you may receive a full reward. Anyone who goes too far and does not abide in the teaching of Christ, does not have God; the one who abides in the teaching, he has both the Father and the Son.

> If anyone comes to you and does not bring this teaching, *do not receive him into your house, and do not give him a greeting; for the one who gives him a greeting participates in his evil deeds* (2 John 1:7-11, emphasis added).

Third, *Don't promise to attend meetings.* Cultists recruit for meetings, counseling sessions, and even retreats. Thousands of young people have naïvely responded to such invitations only to find themselves caught without help in a brainwashing situation. Cultists will attempt to make you feel loved and accepted, keep you up for hours, and lower your defenses to ensnare you into their cultic thinking.

Finally, *Don't be overwhelmed by arguments, personalities, or even physical pressure.* If the situation is getting out of hand, get out. Like Joseph when Potipher's wife approached him, just stand up and leave (see Genesis 39). Many witnessing situations with cultists simply become impossible. Continued efforts or even presence is foolish and possibly dangerous. You are often dealing with an unstable mind capable of almost any form of aberrant behavior or physical aggression. Learn to spot incipient aggressive behavior and know how to cope with it.

Witnessing to a cultist is never easy, and sometimes it's impossible. The probability of conversion to faith in Christ is considerably less than with a person not involved in a cult. People with ministries to people caught in cults know how twisted the human mind can become and how strong Satan is. You might suspect the one to whom you are speaking isn't even listening, then realize that he is simply waiting for you to finish so that he can continue his argument. Spiritual subversion is terrible, and it often requires a special commitment on the part of a Christian to witness to people caught in a maze of unbiblical teachings and practices.

When you have quoted the Word of God to an individual who has been subverted by Satan, you can confidently pray that God will continue to use His Word with that person. No verse of Scripture has ever been quoted without eternal significance. Perhaps you have also had the opportunity to leave a tract or a booklet which, in a moment of rationality, the person may take the time to read.

When it comes to witnessing to people involved in cults, the prelude is prayer and the follow-up is more earnest prayer. God does not promise that the person who is subverted by Satan will recover. Nevertheless, the pointed and compassionate witness brought to the heart of one who is spiritually confused may do its wonderful work. As Tennyson said, "More things are wrought by prayer than this world dreams of."

STUDY QUESTIONS

1. If someone asked you why you are a Christian, what would you say?

2. If he or she followed that up by asking how he or she could become a Christian, what words would you use?

3. Why is remaining close to the Word of God crucial when talking with a cultist?

4. In 1 Timothy 4:7 and 6:20, what advice does Paul have for Timothy regarding discussions with non-Christians?

5. Why should a Christian not attend a cult meeting?

What Lies Ahead

He who is in you is greater than he who is in the world!

We are living in a most interesting time. The events of earth have brought us to the place where it is not inappropriate to suggest we have moved into a period called the "last days." Concerning that time, the Scripture announces that "in the last days difficult times will come" (2 Timothy 3:1). In saying this, the Scripture forever destroys the idea of utopianism—the notion that things will get better and better as we move toward the end. In fact, this very chapter describes these days this way:

> For men will be lovers of self, lovers of money, boastful, arrogant, revilers, disobedient to parents, ungrateful, unholy, unloving, irreconcilable, malicious gossips, without self-control, brutal, haters of good, treacherous, reckless, conceited, lovers of pleasure rather than lovers of God; holding to a form of godliness, although they have denied its power; and avoid such men as these. For among them are those who enter into households and captivate weak women weighed down with sins, led on by various impulses, always learning and never able to come to the knowledge of the truth. . . . But evil men and seducers shall wax worse and worse, deceiving, and being deceived (2 Timothy 3:2-7,13).

We can see that powerful spiritual deception will come upon the world and upon the church in the time of the consummation of history. And we can be grateful that the apostle Paul gives us the very reasons for the perilous times coming. In this passage we have a list of 15 characteristics that will mark the "last days" and actually produce those perilous times. Among the characteristics are blasphemy (showing contempt for God or claiming to be God) and putting on a show of false godliness. Both of these are abundantly evident in the cults of our day, and from them we are supposed to turn away.

From this passage we can see that false religion will continue to take on an external and even beguiling form, but at the core it will be without power, without authority, without truth. It will be cultic rather than Christian. That phenomena will grow because people will be ignorant of the Scripture and ill-versed in the use of the Word of God for spiritual contention. As we consider this, we ought to be motivated as never before to become students of the Bible. The dangerous times that will come upon the world will do so because of violations of the truth of Scripture. Spiritual subversion will take place in the end times because the Word has not been lifted high.

Spiritual Subversion in the Church

We can be well instructed by the words of Christ as He spoke about the end times. The disciples came to Christ in one of those rare moments when they had the opportunity to be alone with Him, and they asked an important question: "Tell us, when will these things be, and what will be the sign of Your coming, and of the end of the age?" (Matthew 24:3). Christ's answer to this question is most instructive. He instantly responded to their concerns by replying, "See to it that no one misleads you. For many will come in My name, saying, 'I am the Christ,' and will mislead many" (Matthew 24:4,5).

This indicates that the first concern of our Lord about the future was the possibility of spiritual subversion in His own ranks. Jesus did not simply predict spiritual deception; He warned His beloved disciples to be careful. There can be no denying that the admonition to "see to it" is Christ's mandate to His disciples—and to all believers between now and the last days of history. The importance of His words is pointed out a bit later when Christ says, "And many false prophets will arise, and will mislead many" (Matthew 24:11).

Having said this, Christ took several minutes to expand on the possibility of spiritual subversion and false doctrine taking over in the ranks of believers: "If anyone says to you, 'Behold, here is the Christ,' or 'There He is,' do not believe him. For false Christs and false prophets will arise and will show great signs and wonders, so as to mislead, if possible, even the elect" (Matthew 24:23,24). Quite obviously the Lord Jesus wanted the faithful of every age to hear and heed His message that the prospect of being subverted was close to each one of us.

Ignoring the Word

We have already seen that Scripture warns us of unusual, intrepid activity on the part of Satan as we move toward the end of the age. The coming satanic church would only be possible if there were an advanced impact of corrupt Christianity that made that entity possible. Paul was, therefore, acutely aware of the dreadful possibilities of false doctrine growing out of ignorance of the Word of God.

It was not just casual remark but grave concern behind Paul's letter to his beloved, yet immature Galatians. "I am amazed that you are so quickly deserting Him who called you by the grace of Christ, for a different gospel; which is really not another; only there are some who are disturbing you, and want to distort the gospel of Christ" (Galatians 1:6,7). Notice the profound concern and resentment Paul had concerning false doctrine in the body of Christ. He even goes on to add, "If any man is preaching to you a gospel contrary to that which you received, let him be accursed" (Galatians 1:9). Surely God intends that every generation of Christians be warned with the same seriousness of what could come upon us if we ignore the teaching of the Word of God.

Satanic theology will one day take over the world, bringing to pass that awful period called "the great tribulation." As we see that day approaching, we must be forewarned and forearmed. False doctrine has fatal consequences for the Christian and the culture. In 1521, standing before the Diet of Worms, Martin Luther said, "Here I stand, I can do no other, so help me God." Out of that statement, that brave conviction, was born the Protestant Reformation. The marvelous truth of justification by faith was carried by glad hearts on winged feet all across northern Germany, the low countries, England, and some of France. The doctrine of justification by faith without the works of the law became the great emphasis of that age. Luther is properly credited with getting people to believe in "the Bible alone, by grace alone, through faith alone." It brought theological research and spiritual revival.

Down through the years, the conviction of the truth of Scripture gradually abated. People became soft on false doctrine and the Reformation faith turned into an ordinary religion. Soon the churches moved the statues back into their places, the crosses and candles back into the sanctuaries, and "Lutheranism" became a stately church rather than an army mighty with banners. The results were tragic.

Later came the teaching and the preaching of Julius Wellhausen and his attendant documentary hypothesis. The result was religious liberalism, which first took hold in northern Germany. Soon liberalism was carried to many places across the world, to the detriment of Protestant Christianity.

The consequences were indeed tragic. Because its Christianity became liberal, the Germans had an empty faith—they had lost the inspiration of the Bible from their liberal traditions. The Word of God became a human book, and the faith became a weakened belief. The German church, as a consequence, did not have the spiritual strength to resist the corruption of the faith. Later it was diluted to the point where it couldn't even resist the rise of Nazism and the presumptuous messianic leadership of Adolph Hitler. The result was that the cult of Nazism took over the land and moved out in an astonishingly presumptuous program of world conquest. Tens of millions of lives later the world reeled in incredulity at the awful, indeed the *satanic* cruelty of the Nazi party. The success of the cult of Nazism was one of the most ruinous developments in the history of the world. Clear biblical exposition, with an attendant warning about spiritual subversion, may well have avoided this.

In the same way, most of the so-called "great religions of the world" are nothing more than *satanic* cults. They have already cost the lives of millions, and they intend to persist in their evil deeds while at the same time aspiring to be masters of earth. "From such turn away" the Bible says. That is our calling. We can do no other. It is my hope that every believer will take seriously the warnings and the admonitions of these pages. If so, the faith can move forward to broad new possibilities. If not, a fearful day of spiritual ruin may well be upon us.

Study Questions

1. What does 2 Timothy 3:1-9 reveal about man's thinking in the last days?

2. Which of these do you see evidenced in our society?

3. How are the warnings in Matthew 24:5,10-14,23,24 meant for us today?

4. How does knowing the truth help us handle lies?

5. What has been the greatest truth you have learned from your time in this book?

1. *Back to Godhead,* no. 61, 1974, p. 24.

2. For an expansion on these themes read David Breese, *Satan's Ten Most Believable Lies.*

3. "We Belong to Krishna," in *Back to Godhead,* no. 46, p. 7.

4. *Back to Godhead,* no. 46, p. 1.

5. *Science and Health,* 1916 ed., 473:15; 332:19; 347:14-15; 332:26-27; 29:32-30:1; 334:10-20; 509:4-7.

6. *Make Sure of All Things,* 1957, p. 207. *Let God Be True,* 1952, pp. 207-10. *Studies in the Scriptures,* 2, p. 129.

7. *The Articles of Faith,* Talmadge, pp. 471-72. *Doctrine and Covenants* 76:24. *Doctrines of Salvation,* Joseph F. Smith, 1, p. 18.

8. Hugh Shearman, *Modern Theosophy,* 1952, pp. 201-02.

9. *Studies in the Scriptures,* V, 54ff. *Make Sure of All Things,* 1957, pp. 191, 386. President Nathan Knorr, *Religion in the 20th Century,* p. 388. *The Kingdom Is at Hand,* p. 507.

10. *Christianity Today,* Nov. 5, 1971, p. 31.

11. It should be noted that in 1997 the leadership of the Worldwide Church of God repented of their cultic ways and heretical theology, moving toward orthodoxy in faith and practice.

12. *Has Religion Betrayed God and Man?* n.d., p. 2.

13. In addition to your church, you'll find excellent resources for witnessing to cultists at *Christian Destiny, Inc.,* P.O. Box C, Hillsboro, KS 67063 and at *Spiritual Counterfeits Project,* P.O. Box 4308, Berkeley, CA 94704. Write for more information.

Dave Breese is president of Christian Destiny, Inc., in Hillsboro, Kansas. He travels approximately 100,000 miles annually in a many-faceted ministry involving preaching, radio and TV, and literature. He is heard on radio and national TV stations on the weekly 30-minute television program and daily 5-minute radio program "Dave Breese Reports."

A member of the Board of Administration of the National Association of Evangelicals, Breese is also the author of *Discover Your Destiny* (Word), *His Infernal Majesty* (Moody), and the national bestseller, *Seven Men Who Rule the World from the Grave* (Moody). Dave and his wife, Carol, live in Kansas and are parents of daughters Lynn and Noelle.

Other Good Harvest House Reading

The Counterfeit Gospel of Mormonism
Frank Beckwith, Norman Geisler, Ron Rhodes, Phil Roberts, and Sandra and Gerald Tanner

Mormons today claim they worship the same God, read the same Bible, and have the same Jesus as all other Christians. But do Mormonism and Christianity really match up? Several highly respected authorities on this subject carefully examine key teachings of Mormonism and Christianity and define the differences between them.

Mind Games
André Kole with Jerry MacGregor

World-renowned magician André Kole, after spending decades studying numerous religious and spiritual wonders, provides clear explanations for supposed psychic miracles and educates readers about the deceptive trickery behind astrology, UFOs, ghosts, mind sciences, and other unexplained phenomena.

Alien Obsession
Ron Rhodes

Are UFOs mentioned in the Bible? What connection do they have with the occult? What is their message to mankind? Using God's Word as a barometer of truth, Ron Rhodes examines the evidence on UFOs to expose their primary agenda and its impact on you.

Darwin's Leap of Faith
John Ankerberg and John Weldon

In light of the magnificent complexity of life and the universe, which takes a bigger leap of faith—believing that our intricate world came about by chance or that it was designed by an intelligent creator? The award-winning team of Ankerberg and Weldon puts the facts surrounding the evolution-creation controversy under the microscope and gives major scientific arguments against the theory of evolution.